BURNED OUT TO LIT UP

DITCH THE GRIND AND RECLAIM YOUR LIFE

CARA E. HOUSER

Parliament
PRESS

Burned Out to Lit Up: Ditch the Grind and Reclaim Your Life

Cover by Madelyn Copperwaite of MC Creative LLC
Editing by Jennifer Crosswhite of Tandem Services LLC
Editing and Marketing by Stephanie Feger of emPower PR Group

First edition, October 2023
ISBN (Paperback): 979-8-9889252-0-0
ISBN (eBook): 979-8-9889252-1-7
Library of Congress Control Number: 2023916793
Created in the United States of America

Learn more about Cara Houser and how her coaching, courses, keynotes, and workshops can support you to step into your power and go from burned out to lit up by visiting www.CaraHouser.com. Special discounts are available on quantity book purchases. Contact hello@carahouser.com for information.

TABLE OF CONTENTS

DEDICATION

To my fellow women trying to be everything to everyone (except ourselves),
who've burned the candle at both ends for too long.

Now is the time to let your light shine.

To my children, Stella and Alden, my life's greatest joy and adventure: how
happy and proud I am to be your mom. You are warm hearted, good
humored, and strong minded, and the world is your oyster. To my husband,
Dave, my soulmate: how grateful I am for the unconditional love we've
shared for nearly three decades and counting.

To my sister, Natalie, my ride or die: how lucky I am to journey through life's
magic, heartbreaks, and joys with you. To my niece and nephews, Mia,
Nolan, and Dominic: I love you to the moon and am so proud of you.

To my dear friend Samantha, my bestie from the start: what a gift you are in
my life and how I've loved our crazy adventures.

You all light up my life. I love you more than words can say and am blessed
to have your loving, supportive, hilarious, delightful souls in my life.

LETTER TO THE READER

Dear Reader,

Welcome! I'm so glad you're here. I can't wait to spend some time with you and help you recover from one of modern life's most prevalent and crushing maladies—burnout.

Like many women, especially full-time working parents and caregivers, I slid down the long slippery slope of being everything to everyone—except myself. Prioritizing sending gifts to distant relatives across the country? Check. Signing up to volunteer for one more school or sports thing for the kids? Check. Ditching kickboxing class again to help meet an "emergency deadline" (which resulted from someone else's poor planning) that just popped up at work? Check. Engaging in hours of unpaid cultural or domestic labor for the good of society and community? Check. You get the picture.

One choice at a time, I betrayed myself and my own needs in favor of trying to do multiple full-time jobs in the time (and for the price) of one. Until one day I realized I had become a dried-up raisin of the robust, energetic, creative, fun, kickass person I once was. I had become so fried that I had no idea how to even begin to claw my way out and not an ounce of energy to figure it out. Even looking for the resources to help myself out of this hole seemed impossible. I ended up in such a bad place that I needed to take a leave from work for the sake of my physical and mental health, embarking on what would become a nearly two-year hiatus (later known as my sabbatical).

My journey out of burnout and into rich, joy-filled, full-bodied living required me to get really clear on the fact that even amid life's responsibilities of work and family, remaining true to myself is an essential ingredient for a thriving life. I also learned that I *need* the basic building blocks of mental and physical well-being, just like all humans do. I need a certain amount of sleep, outdoor exercise, balanced nutrition, and time to explore and enjoy life in order to function.

Having requirements for well-being does not make me soft or weak, and these are not fun "extras" that get slotted in if there's a bit of time at the end of my endless to-do list or if someone else gives me a hall pass. As most of us know, there's *never* time at the end of the to-do list, and it's often filled with expectations and demands from the outside world. No one is going to give us permission to live our own lives; it's not even their job to do so.

While recovering from my own burnout, I test-drove resources, books, classes, and practices, and I've distilled the greatest hits so you can get down to the restorative business of your recovery from burnout. With specific and tested guidance, compelling stories, and applied, practical wisdom, I will guide you from soul-crushing burnout, through self-care, all the way to the magic of self-possession.

I learned the more I nourished myself inside and out, the more I had to give to my family, my work, and the world—and the opposite is also true. I learned how to ditch the weight of external expectations and build a healthy foundation based on openness to possibility, restoring my core self, and doing more of what lights me up with the people and things that matter most. I reclaimed my life, and you can too.

I can't promise this journey will be free of pain and tears, but I've done my very best to include only the most useful resources, strategies, and practices to make it as accessible, nurturing, and even fun as possible. I *can* assure you this journey of restoration and reconnection with yourself will be one of the most worthwhile of your life. At the end, you'll find yourself bursting with ideas and energy and reveling in the bold technicolor life you were born to live.

You got this.

Cara Estelle Houser

INTRODUCTION

Don't ask what the world needs. Ask what makes you come alive and go do it.
Because what the world needs is people who have come alive.
— Howard Thurman

BURNOUT IS THE NEWEST GLOBAL PANDEMIC

Did you know that a 2018 Deloitte study found that 77% of Americans report experiencing burnout within the previous year? And by 2023, a study by Zippia reports that number has risen to 89%. The World Health Organization, Mayo Clinic and other health organizations also acknowledge burnout as a widespread problem, although they vary on defining it and are somewhat vague on dealing with it.

If you're a mid-career woman and have been hacking your way through American work culture for a while, I'm willing to bet that percentage is even higher (ensnaring nearly everyone), and that you're experiencing all the wonderful things that accompany burnout— feeling overwhelmed, undervalued, maybe even trapped, and lost as to what to do about it. I'll bet you've spent more time than you care to count trying to be everything to everyone (family, friends, the neighbor down the street, your boss, culture, church, community) with little regard to your own needs or identity. I see you; I was you, and I can help you get yourself out.

Kickass humans like you want autonomy, power, possibility, and purpose in their lives, and they want to feel alive, energized, lit-up, and ready to make an impact in the world.

They want to spend their precious and limited time, energy, and resources on the people and things that matter most. I'd venture to say that not only are you a kickass human, but you know there's more to life than barely surviving, buried under your endless to-do lists, thinking someday you'll finally have a scrap of time to restore yourself and pursue that passion project that's been simmering beneath the surface for years, wondering when you'll get the chance to find out what else is out there for you.

If this inner stirring started as a whisper, then became a declarative sentence, and has now escalated to a primal scream, don't worry; you're in good company. Bronnie Ware wrote a somewhat gut-wrenching book called *The Top Five Regrets of the Dying*. These regrets are:

1. "I wish I'd had the courage to live a life true to myself, not the life others expected of me."
2. "I wish I hadn't worked so hard."
3. "I wish I'd had the courage to express my feelings."
4. "I wish I had stayed in touch with my friends."
5. "I wish I had let myself be happier."

Number one says it all, and the others flow from it. Most people spend too much time and energy worrying about everyone else's expectations, opinions, and business, and too little time getting clear on how *they* feel and what matters most to *them*, and then moving toward it—one thought, choice, action, and habit at a time.

For women, the problem is even more acute, since most of us have been conditioned from birth to be caring, accommodating to a fault, and even to ignore our own needs and desires in favor of serving others and the communities we live in. This tees us up perfectly to play roles written by others rather than claiming the starring role in our own lives. The pressure to do this is intense, and even if you're a stubborn ox like me, it's a relatively easy habit trap to fall into.

Ask yourself: what would you regret having not spent more time on or not having done if your life ended before you had a chance to do it? When have you too heavily favored saving joy and money for the future versus enjoying your life and the people in it now?

AN INVITATION

If you picked up this book, you're probably a dream family member, employee, volunteer, and an all-around excellent human doing all the "right things." I suspect you've read lots of leadership and personal development books and tried all the shortcuts Google can cough up to save time, be efficient, and do it all without breaking a sweat.

In order to squeeze all of this in, you've likely ditched most, if not all of the things that would support your well-being or aid your resilience (like nutrition, exercise, sleep, spiritual practice, hobbies, time with loved ones, time with friends, unstructured down time, and anything that might be construed as frivolous or fun.) Once you've trotted down this shit-strewn path for a while, burnout, rage, grief, self-blame, ill physical health, mental health challenges, and soul-crushing exhaustion are inevitable.

Take heart; you are not alone. The majority of midlife women in demanding careers feel the same way, and it's not a result of having done anything "wrong." It's a result of doing it all so "right" and then realizing the only thing wrong was the insanely unachievable set of expectations you somehow signed on to.

We dream of an *Eat, Pray, Love*-style escape like Julia Roberts had in the movie, where we drop everything, travel to exotic places, and eat, pray, and love ourselves into a glowing state of well-being—but we have bills, responsibilities, and loved ones at home, and we suspect the things that need attention (mindset, self-worth, self-love, relationship issues, unhealthy habits or coping mechanisms, physical and mental health challenges) will follow us abroad anyway.

You've tried but haven't figured out how to give yourself the time, space, and resources to slow down. I invite you to think differently and chart a new course that's aligned with your values and what you actually want out of life. Or that you *would* want if you took the time to dig deep and find out.

You'd also love for people to see you're exhausted, to quit asking for stuff, and to back the hell off. Yet you're scared to be the one to insist on making these changes, which you know will cause a stir you don't feel like dealing with. After all, isn't *everyone* fried? Do you really deserve a break? You probably don't have it *that* bad, do you? Shouldn't you just suck it up and soldier along?

Why can't someone just cough up the freakin' playbook already!

Well, I have excellent news for you. The next nine chapters contain just that. It *is* possible to reclaim yourself in body, mind, and spirit, and recenter your life around who and what matters most to you without breaking the bank, falling into an existential abyss, or losing what's left of what's holding you together. You can create a multidimensional, badass life that you don't need to escape from.

I can't wait to guide you through the distilled and curated process I used and that I now help other women navigate. It will help you go from self-neglect, through self-care, to the powerful state of self-possession. No need to wait for a crash during an overdue vacation, illness, or emergency, or that long-fabled retirement, which many people reach running on fumes only to discover they've not nurtured their health, important relationships, or passions, and don't really know how to live fully outside the box of their prescribed work and societal roles.

The very best part about this journey is that it's the opposite of zero sum. It's the truest win-win I know.

When we learn to nourish ourselves inside and out, to give ourselves respect, compassion, and love, we are exponentially better-equipped not only to show up whole and happy for our loved ones and work, but to give these gifts to others in our lives, radiating our inner light as we go.

TOUGH LESSONS FROM THE SCHOOL OF LIFE

I spent twenty years learning how to survive and ultimately thrive in the ultra-male, 24/7, meat grinder field of real estate development. It's an "always on" business, in which it is a peculiar badge of honor to be so "busy" as to have few, if any, other priorities in life. During that time, my teams produced over 3,000 homes in the San Francisco Bay Area, creating over $1.5 billion in value. If you can develop housing in the Bay Area (where everyone says they want to support equitable opportunities for others to live, learn, and work in our beautiful region, but no one wants any more actual neighbors or buildings anywhere near their house and will fight tooth and nail to keep them out), you can smash just about any hurdle in your path.

After slogging away for the first fifteen years, doing all (most? some?) of the things working parents are "supposed" to do, with two children and a crushing set of expectations from myself, work, home, and beyond, I hit a nasty wall caused by years of built-up exhaustion and overload, and ultimately a family health emergency.

These factors reached a boiling point that caused me to quit my job and embark on a career break of unknown duration to figure out how to heal myself inside and out so I could show up as the person, mom, wife, sister, friend, and professional I wanted to be.

I will share with you how I went from an anxiety-ridden shell of myself to reconnecting with my intrinsic value and values, ensuring my time and energy are focused intentionally on the people and things that matter most (including me).

As I recovered from burnout, I got my mojo back, and with it plenty of motivation to get back in the game of work. By shifting my perspective, strategy, and approach, I rebuilt my career with far more autonomy and purpose. Learning I had the power to set my own rules of engagement with the world was a watershed moment; I just had to learn how to use it.

Bursting with ideas and inspiration, I started a consulting business in my field and worked on many exciting projects with terrific clients, chosen based on shared purpose and mutual benefit. I was able to set appropriate boundaries around work and other demands and protect precious time to raise my family and treat my own needs like they actually mattered, despite what others may have thought.

Now I'm a career strategist and empowerment coach, and I help high-impact women leaders step into their power and go from burned out to lit up. Clients hone their ability to see and articulate their value (and values) and tap into their power, possibility, and purpose to pursue what matters most to them in their lives and careers. Fuck off, hustle culture. Hello rich, full-bodied, joy-filled life.

It's a gift to work with incredible and inspiring clients, providing thought partnership, strategic insight, clarity on value and values, healthy mindset practice, new chapter exploration, career acceleration support, and accountability. The kind we all need from time to time, especially when in a period of growth or transition.

HOW TO NAVIGATE THIS BOOK

The suggested cadence for this book is one week per chapter—and the first week is almost in the bag! Each chapter is followed by a few Reflection Activities: questions, ideas, or activities to help you apply the concepts to your own life in meaningful ways for you. These Reflection Activities are also compiled at the end of the book in case you want to reference them all together. It will be helpful to have a lovely journal and favorite pen or pencil to use for these activities. Or you can go to www.CaraHouser.com to print out a free PDF workbook of all the Reflection Activities in this book.

Ready to go from burned out to lit up? Let's go!

REFLECTION ACTIVITIES

Write yourself a letter, dated ten weeks out from now, about how you'll feel, who you'll be, and what you'll do after this journey. It is to be written in the past tense, as though these things have already come to pass. In your letter, describe:

- What you've learned, experienced, and applied to your life.
- The ways your life has been positively impacted and transformed.
- How you feel about yourself and the year to come.

IT'S GETTING HOT IN HERE

You must be ready to burn yourself in your own flame; how could you rise
anew if you have not first become ashes?
— Friedrich Nietzsche, *Thus Spoke Zarathustra*

My family says I'm a natural meerkat—always on the lookout for threats on the horizon and ready to protect loved ones from attack. While this vigilance has come in handy at times in helping avoid disaster or to problem-solve my way out of sticky situations both personally and professionally, extreme vigilance is debilitating, exhausting, and ultimately ineffective. It's simply impossible to anticipate and defuse every potential landmine on the horizon, thereby paving the way for risk-free, daisy-skipping, Frappuccino-sipping living. Not that it stopped me from trying.

When my son was five and my daughter was seven, I was deep in physical, mental, and even spiritual exhaustion. My natural stress setpoint was so high I barely noticed how truly out of balance I'd become. Personality-wise, I actually hate expending energy on anticipating the worst and had worn myself down to a charcoal nub trying to inhabit a mindset that was incompatible with my soul. I love an adventure and finding new and more interesting ways to solve problems and live out loud. Even so, I'd put that part of me in an airtight box and systematically chopped just about everything out of my daily life that could have brought me rest, health, or resilience—all in pursuit of getting it all done, being all things to all people, and somehow crushing it all in style.

Anyone who has practiced burning the candle at both ends for any period of time will be familiar with what happens when we routinely neglect ourselves.

We Gen X women in particular were sold a bill of goods. We're the first generation of women raised on the shoulder-pad-wearing, *Working Girl* movie-watching notion that we could participate in the world of paid work on equal footing. The fine print was that we were still expected to perform *all* the full-time, unpaid, domestic labor we were already doing as well, which includes but is not limited to: running household affairs from chores to cooking to shopping to planning to childbearing to childrearing to taking care of our aging parents to volunteering at the PTA, food bank, church, and anywhere else that relies on our free labor to exist and invisibly lubricate the social and philanthropic workings of society, to managing any and all social interactions, to making sure all holidays, birthdays, and other rituals are stocked, fun, and enriching, to "maintaining ourselves" and looking fabulous while doing it!

Here's a depressing look at what doing two full-time jobs at the same time looks like:

- Sleeping like crap and developing permanent dark eye bags, creaky joints, and the bone-deep exhaustion it seems like only death can relieve.

- Spending little-to-no time nurturing relationships outside your immediate household (and not feeling like you're crushing those either at times).
- Eating only things that take a max of ten to fifteen minutes to whip up.
- Declining to do most things that seem frivolous or like a waste of time (i.e. fun).
- Dragging your ragged self into work less and less confident of your ability to do anything well. After all, no one is particularly pleased with your "half-assed" performance.
- Snapping at people and immediately feeling bad about yourself for having an emotion.
- Quitting healthy and/or relaxing habits—like swimming, crafting, reading the Sunday paper, hiking in nature, journaling, practicing mindfulness, having a spiritual practice, reading anything not related to work or childrearing—since you "don't have time" for you.
- Tolerating the thoughts, actions, habits, people, and places that constantly drain your will to live, thinking that good, loving people like you should put up with crap as an act of loyalty and commitment.
- Forgetting you ever wanted to pursue anything else, like learning another language or guitar, making pottery, starting a band, or traveling more.
- Collapsing into a heap at night and looking forward to sleep like it's the greatest part of your day.
- Secretly hoping you'll develop a serious medical condition that requires hospitalization so you can escape it all and have everyone back the fuck off for once.

I was in that brittle and fried state when a family emergency happened. It laid bare the fact that, despite our best efforts, we can still get ourselves into some very bad places, to the detriment of not only ourselves but also to those around us.

One blizzardy February night, we were visiting friends in a small mountain town where we'd traveled for a weekend visit. We were in charge of dinner for the crowd, which included another family.

In the frenzy of making the meal and keeping an eye on the kids—and I'm sure tracking a hundred other things in my unpleasantly busy brain—we'd failed to inform the other guests that our son had a life-threatening nut allergy or ask what they'd brought to share.

All the kids finished eating quickly and scampered off to play, taking the tray of nut-filled brownies with them (unbeknown to us). Even though he was only five, my son was well-versed in having a food allergy. He was used to asking what is in desserts at school birthday parties before partaking, for example, but he'd never seen brownies with tiny bits of walnuts before (he thought they were white chocolate chips) and dug in.

Our daughter came booking up the stairs to tell us she thought her brother had eaten nuts, and we went into emergency mode (for me it looked like more of a freak-out mode). When asked how he felt moments later, my son said his throat felt weird and tight, a sign of anaphylaxis, and I think I felt my soul flee my body for a moment. We grabbed the baby Benadryl and administered the EpiPen auto injector shot into his thigh while our hosts called 911.

The snowstorm was horrible, and the house was remote, so it would be a while for the ambulance to arrive, and more time to get to a hospital. As the minutes dragged by, I struggled mightily to mask the growing panic in my body and mind, since it was only a matter of time until the EpiPen's effects wore off. We needed to get to the hospital fast.

When the ambulance finally arrived, my son and I were hustled in, and our family and friends followed behind. He was so sleepy from the effects of medication I felt the urge to continually check that he was breathing all the way during our interminable ride. We made it, thank God. He was treated, and we were sent back to the house with more medication to get through the next volatile and vigilant twenty-four hours.

I remember sobbing on our friends' couch the next morning, asking how I'd allowed myself to get so depleted that I failed to protect my child. Huge helpings of guilt, self-blame, and shame accompanied the fear and stress that were still there from the night before—an emotional hell cocktail.

I had no idea how I got so burned out and even less of a clue how to come back to life.

I admitted through ugly cries that sent the kids running to far corners of the house that my attempts at doing it all were doing me in and I didn't know how to fix it.

At that moment, my friend suggested a concept that would not just be game-changing for me but would be life-altering for so many women I've been able to help since. "A sabbatical could be a place to start," she noted, observing that I needed to step away, reflect, evaluate, and make some changes.

At first, I thought sabbaticals were only for pastors and professors, not for regular people like us. Then I doubted I *deserved* this or could do it without permission from others in my life. Indeed many folks (family, coworkers, the lady at the corner store), loudly (and uninvitedly!) voiced their fears about the demise of my career and probably my life.

How would I get a real job again with a big resume gap? I'd be labeled as someone who couldn't take the pressure. How would we live on one salary and meet our financial obligations and goals?

These are the terrifying stories we tell ourselves that keep our wings clipped down tight, that keep us assuming there are no "realistic" possibilities or options to really start living (versus surviving).

Those voices of doom were loud inside me too. I'd grown up in very modest circumstances, and fears around financial security were never far from my mind. For this reason, I always had money squirrelled away and a hefty plan B in case of disaster. But my mental and physical state at the time were in such dire straits that they demanded I act and take real responsibility for my life choices.

So I pushed forward and planned with my partner-in-crime (my husband, Dave) to reclaim my life and make the positive impact on our family life I so desperately longed for. I leaned hard into faith that it would work out even though I didn't yet have the answers, and I reminded myself of all the times I'd been resourceful and resilient in the past. I could do this. I had everything I needed within me to take a big leap and you do too.

SIGNS, SIGNS, EVERYWHERE THE SIGNS

Although I didn't recognize it at the time, the signs of extreme exhaustion and burnout were bubbling up long before an emergency caused such a disruption in what I now see was my extremely frayed, barely surviving nervous system. I knew I was stressed, but wasn't everyone in this phase of life? Why was I special? Most folks I knew were full-time working parents or caregivers in demanding jobs, and the general sense of running a hundred miles per hour, being too busy, and constantly trying to catch up was as common as it was boring.

On one particularly intense day at work, I yelled (yes, top-of-my-lungs yelled) at one of our commercial tenants in a new project we'd developed who was causing friction with other businesses in the building with her repeatedly blaring music. She seemed to care not a bit about the impact of her actions, which drove me nuts, and instead of trying other methods of communication to get through to her, I just went straight to level 11.

I realized my mistake immediately, was highly embarrassed, and ended up having to "tell on" myself to my boss to reluctantly admit my behavior. I even called the tenant to offer an apology a few hours later. Her behavior was problematic and did need to be addressed, but it's never appropriate to yell at people, however cathartic it may feel for a fleeting moment.

The expectation that women elegantly perform two full-time jobs (and being criticized for doing neither "right") is crushing.

Showing up full of Mary Poppins poise, grace, style, and humor feels way out of reach when your head is barely above water in the river of shit you are muddling through. I longed for some of that Mary Poppins swagger, like when the exasperated Mr. Banks demands an explanation of her, and she declares that she never explains anything, and floats away up the stairs.

I thought I knew better, but I still fell right into the trap. Like a slow-motion free fall over several years and several thousand small self-betrayals, I had descended into the habit of putting everything else first, and abandoning responsibility for my own well-being.

One by one, I moved all the things that supported my physical and mental well-being down on my to-do list until they were so low I never actually got to them. I relegated them to the pile of optional nice-to-haves, instead of the essential necessities for survival that they are. Eventually I forgot they even existed, struggled to recall the things I once liked or found relaxing, and wondered whether I had personal interests at all.

LIFE-WORK BALANCE, NOT WORK-LIFE BALANCE— FRAMING IS EVERYTHING

I've come to loathe the notion of work-life balance as it has become a torture chamber for people trying in vain to get that "balance right," as though the elusive state is but one book, meditation, or massage away. It's a lose-lose scenario, and it subconsciously elevates one of life's activities (work) above all others. Sadly, it's perfectly fitting in America, where most folks *do* put work above health, family, fun, everything (and are shamed or made to feel like lazy bums if they don't).

You may have heard this elsewhere or concluded it on your own, but there's no way to get that work-life balance "right" between societal demands and career. It's a trap to even think balance is possible by being even more efficient, sacrificing even more of ourselves and our basic human needs. This sacrifice is a recipe for so much stress and pain.

Work-life balance is a con, and we must reject it in order to reclaim our inner power and our lives—body, mind, and spirit.

For me, this realization was astonishingly liberating. It allowed me to rebuild my life without the pressure and shame of feeling like a failure so I could choose my priorities consciously, set boundaries, and show up more freely, authentically, and joyfully in all realms of life.

It is why I now refer to this lovely balancing act as life-work balance, a simple reordering that makes all the difference. I've learned that the way to power, possibility, and purpose lies in crafting a lifestyle meant for actual human living and thriving, one where *life* comes before *work* and work is simply one of many elements of a rich and full life.

You know the best part? When ordered properly, both the life and the work are so much better for it. When I'm centered and fulfilled in my multidimensional life, my work is more creative and higher quality, and I show up with the humanity needed to connect with others and lead high performing teams where people are seen and contribute their best. And I'm so much more relaxed and fulfilled in my personal life, showing up with more patience and care for those most important to me. What a win-win.

This lifestyle can take many forms and can exist within organizations as well as among solopreneurs. With hybrid work arrangements and four-day workweeks becoming more prevalent, there are more opportunities than ever to get creative with ordering our habits, days, and lives in service of crafting a life worth living.

Many "9-5ers" work far more than eight hours a day and are essentially on call 24/7 thanks to the wonders of technology. Even if their work is literally saving lives, (which, let's face it, most of us are not), every human being requires time away to recharge and create, days off to recover, and a life complete with interesting pursuits and meaningful relationships. I mean, even surgeons get days off.

It's still deeply ingrained in American work culture, though, that if you don't give 100 percent plus to your paid work (thereby abdicating responsibility for the rest of your life), you are not truly committed. This is horrendous and an outright lie.

It's the chief explanation for the epidemic of burnout, and it's related to the three other ugly horsemen of the hustle apocalypse: poor health, depression, and emptiness. The bottom line is that it's not possible to maintain a healthy lifestyle or relationships when activities related to the other elements of your life are nowhere to be found on your to-do list.

Some statistics: the Harvard Business Review estimates that annual healthcare spending alone due to workplace burnout is anywhere from $125 billion to $190 billion—and this doesn't even include lost work hours due to illness. Ironically, US employees are reluctant to take the paid time off they've earned to rest, vacation, and recharge for fear of seeming uncommitted, but then they have to take those days off (and more) due to the resulting physical and mental health problems. Not to mention that a sick day to crawl out of exhaustion-induced illness is a pathetic replacement for a vacation day at the beach, with friends, or even binging movies and ice cream with your family on the couch.

I have learned the hard way to put myself and my loved ones high on my to-do list—like we actually matter—and then keep my commitments to both. I've learned to create protective guardrails around these activities and not let them slip off the list or get overwritten every time an "urgent" external demand makes its way onto my radar.

After all, if you don't decide you and your loved ones matter and act accordingly, who will? And none of us are getting any younger, so each day we push away ourselves and our partners, kids, and dreams is one less day we'll ever have to enjoy them.

WHAT BURNOUT IS AND ISN'T

Burnout is not a sign of doing things wrong. It is a sign of hustling and grinding so freaking hard to do everything "right" and still feeling like a failure.

The overwhelming stress and exhaustion run so deep that it's hard to imagine ever getting enough rest to come back to life. Burnout creates disconnection—from ourselves, our needs, our interests, and our relationships with others that matter most in our lives.

Here's a truth bomb for you: You can't fail at something that was never even possible anyway.

So, let's start there. You've not failed to get here. You're probably the kind of person who works their lil' fingers to the bone to do right by people and the world—so take a load off, ma'am. Please and thank you.

Most people get to crisis before they get serious about making changes for their own well-being. But the sooner you can start turning the cargo ship of unsustainable habits and mindsets around, the quicker your recovery will be.

Let's face it, it's tough to do maintenance on a car when it's been totaled. Not that *you* are totaled—but you're likely experiencing some form of burnout, from mid-level to severe, and you're in need of some serious restoration. Once your reserves are depleted and your nerves are fried to a crisp, it's tough to even cope with the basic stressors that come with everyday living, much less evaluate, design, and execute a plan to help get yourself out of burnout and back into full-bodied living.

You've come to the right place. We're going to rip out the weeds of doing it all *right* that got us here and source and plant seeds of doing it *right for us*, for *our* healthy new beginning.

HUSTLE, GRIND, AND THE FROG

If you're looking to place blame, look no further than the twin set of culture culprits hiding in plain sight: Hustle and Grind. In American work culture—especially in certain industries like commercial real estate, tech, law, and finance—it's common to feel the need to be constantly busy and oversubscribed to the point where health, relationships, and anything resembling joy degenerate until they are eventually snuffed out. In the Deloitte and Zippia studies mentioned earlier, 77 percent and 89 percent of Americans reported being burned out, respectively. Is it really a mystery why?

It's in the water, as they say. These *values* of burning yourself down to ash are prime ingredients in the larger soup of work culture we all swim in.

In an environment where people often must move heaven and earth to regain even the most basic forms of autonomy over their work and any semblance of life-work balance, burnout is all but inevitable. Left unchecked, it damages physical and mental health and can even be life-threatening.

A friend of mine's company division was driven so hard for so long that she developed significant health issues and had to take a leave of absence to recover. Her boss's response after years of bone-crushing effort and well documented success? "You can't cut it here and should start looking for another position."

At her job and many others, we've gotten to a place where loyalty runs one way only; employees are expected to endure all manner of indignity and never bat an eye (or leave for a better opportunity), but the minute profit dips a tiny bit for the folks at the top, workers are fired without so much as a note telling them so, left to learn they don't work there anymore when their keycard and server access are deactivated.

If you're working for a company with an important mission, wise and long-term-thinking leaders, and a focus on excellence and shared success, this section won't resonate as much. Thank goodness there are work environments illustrating how to do it right. These organizations not only tend to attract fabulous folks to their teams, but they also produce consistently admirable results.

For everyone else though, burnout is a common outcome of hustle and grind culture. Even though leadership knows it exists, has power to address it, and often gives lip service to giving a shit about it, they won't. If you don't take control yourself, you'll eventually come face-to-face with the dismal reality that at the end of the day you are a simply a pawn in a game that sees you as a resource to use up and spit out at their convenience.

We may think we know better, and burnout can't happen to us (I know I did). But it does—to most people at some point in life. It creeps up like the proverbial frog in slowly boiling water. As the pot gets incrementally warmer, the frog adapts, and its emergency ejection system never kicks into place. It is boiled alive.

We, too, can be lulled into a false sense of comfort as the demands on our time and energy from paid work, caretaking, the demands of culture and basic adulting, and other sources slowly ramp up. Bit by bit, we ditch every single thing that has nurtured us, thinking we don't have time. Thinking that if we are just a little more efficient, a little faster, a little better at multitasking, maybe we can cram that whole damn list in, but it never happens.

> Once the things that nurture us are gone, things get ugly real fast, and stay ugly until we realize what's at the root of the issue and take steps toward recovery.

That, my friends, is a quick primer on what I've come to call old burnout—the burnout that results from trying to fit forty-eight hours of stuff into twenty-four hours. New burnout has all the features of old burnout but adds even more to them: technology, followed by time-consuming and expensive regimens.

The wonders of technology, while they can be convenient and offer efficiency and new ways to communicate, also make us accessible to work and social pressures 24/7. We have to be very explicit about setting boundaries in order to protect even a sliver of time to rest.

People who do set boundaries are often considered slackers at work and luddites at home. Just ask my teenagers. Smartphones, with news and social media apps ready to suck our weary souls into hopeless oblivion at the click of a button, are also exquisitely well designed to be addictive energy and attention suckers.

You know that not-so-subtle expectation that women remain youthful and cheerful in body and mind, wrinkle-free, with perfectly coifed (never gray) hair? The self-care industry has flourished in recent years with brilliant ways to profit by suggesting that if we're not doing our jobs gorgeously, maybe there's something wrong with us. Maybe we should just take up meditation, yoga, gratitude journaling, reiki, aromatherapy, or ice baths to balance ourselves. Perhaps lip filler, liposuction, or Botox might fix us, or at least make us look less hag like.

SELF-POSSESSION IS THE KEY

Burnout recovery is the journey from self-neglect, through self-care, all the way to self-possession.

Many of us have been conditioned to put everything else first (self-neglect). We then layer on more—sometimes lovely and helpful, sometimes expensive and useless—stuff to do (self-care) before mastering self-possession (where we are driven by internal values and live true to ourselves).

Self-possession is the pot of gold at the end of the rainbow, and it's also buried deep inside you right now, waiting to be set free.

Self-neglect looks like people-pleasing, perfectionism, ignoring your own needs and desires, and otherwise hustling for approval from external sources. But trust me, they'll never be satisfied anyway, even if we always put them first.

Self-care, as we've come to know it, has been largely co-opted by the marketplace, which has commodified well-being, taking this golden opportunity to double down on the notion that if we just bought this thing or did that practice, we'd be fresh as a flower. American culture makes it clear that time not spent doing paid work is not that important, and then once you're an exhausted bag of bones, it sells your well-being back to you. It has added more for our already-torched brains and budgets to do and buy. Instead of feeling restored, we are left feeling even more broken, broke, and too tired to even be pissed about it anymore.

If we define self-care as the thoughts, actions, and habits that support our well-being, it's wonderful and essential. These are the things you do to take tender, loving care of yourself inside and out, and ideally are a regular part of your life. They are also the things we often dump the minute our schedules get packed with working, caregiving, and managing the domestic realm. Even when we do all of this, though, it is still not enough.

The ultimate tool for combating burnout is self-possession, not self-care. Self-possession is about just that: being in possession of our own self, inside and out. Our well-being is intrinsic to us, and ours to claim and cultivate at any time. It's about being deeply connected to our intuition, to our values, and to what lights us up. It's also about knowing, respecting, and loving ourselves such that our thoughts, actions, and habits are in alignment with our internal values.

In this way of being, we don't waste time, energy, or money on things that don't really matter. Self-possession is achieved through recognizing how we unwittingly give our personal power away (often by hustling for external validation) and reclaiming it.

Burnout recovery is not truly possible without a deeply rooted sense of self-possession, of belonging to ourselves—a sense that our well-being, our souls, cannot be bought or sold, and that our value is innate to us. It cannot be given by others or taken away.

We can give ourselves love, grace, and approval now, firmly rooted in our own foundation of self-worth and the life we build to show we do indeed value ourselves. We need to move from disconnection and self-neglect to reconnection with our core value and values, including and then moving beyond self-care, ultimately pursuing the freedom of self-possession and the rich, full-bodied, joy-filled life that awaits us there.

THE PLAYBOOK

This passage to self-possession involves learning how to incorporate the following elements into our lives here and now, wherever we are. The following chapters will guide you through each phase of the journey, which is split broadly into three sections. Since we've already established that your plate is far too full of (sometimes unwanted) buffet items, we start with getting rid of what doesn't serve us at this phase of our lives, continue with adding in what does, and then cementing it in with sustaining practices so we enjoy lasting benefit.

Chapters 2-4: Making space—physically, mentally, emotionally, and in our schedules and setting boundaries necessary to hold space for what really matters to us.

Chapters 5-7: Rebuilding—discovering and consciously incorporating the mindsets, practices, and habits that best serve our well-being into our everyday lives.

Chapters 8-9: Sustaining—cultivating resilience and joy in an ongoing manner so we can sustain the rich, joyful, and connected lifestyles we've created, and so this experience doesn't join the dust heap of other transformations we've tried to incorporate into our lives in the past.

REFLECTION ACTIVITIES

- Consider how you are feeling now. What does burnout look and feel like to you?
- Consider how you hope to feel by the end of this book. Jot your thoughts down.
- As you reflect on your life, take inventory of what's most important to you. How do your priorities and values align with how you spend your time?
- Read two poems by Mary Oliver: "The Journey" and "Wild Geese."

2

MAKE PHYSICAL SPACE

Have nothing in your houses that you do not know to be beautiful or believe to be useful.
— William Morris

One of the first things I did when I took a sabbatical was apply the Kon Mari method (details to come) of tidying up to my house. Let me tell you, Marie Kondo was right. Purging physical things in your dwelling and working spaces does open up space in your head to think more clearly and to be open to new possibilities that were formerly invisible to you. Marie walks her readers through not just the technical aspects of this work, but also the mental and emotional, which for some people (like me!) are the hardest parts and the ones that prevent us from doing it in the first place.

Even though my kids were out of diapers when I did the first purge of our little house, I found that we still had boxes of them stored in the back of the closet. Yikes! As I parted with baby carriers, strollers, and toddler toys, I reminisced about time, struck by how fleeting it was, and worried I hadn't relished their younger years as thoroughly as I might have due to the whirlwind of staying ahead of the bills, keeping our health insurance during a nasty recession, and meeting the demands of everyone and everything else.

Regret is a real bully, and some days threatened to pull me under the waves.

It often demanded to revisit every trade-off or decision I'd ever made to determine whether it was the right one, and it made sure I knew my current emotional turmoil was 100 percent my own making.

I'd longed for more time with my kids, to really soak up every minute of their childhood, to connect with them in an unhurried way, and to be the best mom I could be, and here was my golden opportunity to wipe the schedule slate clean and intentionally fill it with more time with them, on healing myself, and on rebuilding my life in the direction my heart desired. The more I did this, the more clarity I gained on how to live in alignment with my values and what (and who) mattered most to me. My anxiety decreased and I felt at greater peace, more relaxed, and more present.

Decluttering helped me work through some of that regret and grief and refocus my mind toward gratitude for all the time, opportunities, and gifts I'd received up to that moment; for the time I was now taking to reconnect with my family, my home, and myself; and for the adventures glittering in the distance.

Creating physical space by releasing the unnecessary possessions tethering me to earlier times allowed me to dream a bit about how my next chapter might look, how I might create a life outside the rules and race of hustle culture, and to even start to feel excited about the process. This was the beginning of a journey of exploring new pathways that would invite more joy, autonomy, and purpose in my life.

A ROOM OF ONE'S OWN

As part of my decluttering process, I also looked at each space for possibilities to repurpose it into something more useful, delightful, or both. In Virginia Woolf's famous essay "A Room of One's Own," she talks about how women's freedom of thought, expression, and participation in society are severely limited without personal physical space of their own to work and explore. The economic and social limitations on women were so extreme at the time that very few roles were available to them, and the roles available involved abdication of the self in service of others.

I decided to carve out such a space in the little 1940s era Cape Cod-style two-bedroom, one-bathroom house our family of four cozily shared and found it to be as essential as Woolf said it was. Luckily a literal room is not required to serve this purpose, as I discovered. Such "rooms" can come in various shapes and sizes, so if space is scarce for you, think a bit on where you might create a workable nook. After all, if Harry Potter could live in the cupboard under the stairs and babies in the old days could sleep in dresser drawers, I could figure out something.

I'd heard of folks converting closets to offices, but closets in '40s homes assumed you had three outfits and one pair of shoes, so that was out for us. We did have an underutilized three-foot by five-foot dormer window in our bedroom, though, which I repurposed as my office. Dave built me a snug-fitting desktop at standing height and secured it to the wall, and I got one of those walking treadmills that you can get for a few hundred bucks on Amazon.

My former boss had gotten similar ones for us in our office after declaring that "sitting is the new smoking" and that we needed to stand or walk while working to avoid certain early death, and I loved it. It's the only true multitasking I've ever encountered; you really can take calls and work on your computer while walking, and for several years at work, that was the only exercise I got on weekdays aside from the everyday stuff like an evening play session at the park with kids or running to Target or the grocery store.

I also painted the walls, put up artwork from my kids and others, installed bulletin boards to post pictures and track goals and progress, and added a curtain to serve as a gentle reminder that this space was off-limits to the rest of the family. I had the greatest 15-square-foot office ever. Having a spot where you can store your work, creative supplies, hobby materials, and even household admin stuff you're dealing with and not have them moved, bothered, or lost is a gift. My little office with a laptop computer became ground zero for my first consulting business eighteen months later.

IT'S NOT ABOUT EFFICIENCY; IT'S ABOUT PRIORITIES AND CURATION

I'm sure you know a thing or two about balancing way too many plates at once or keeping all the fiery batons in the air, Miss Congeniality-style. Maybe you've optimized your time management skills and focus like a laser when you're at the office, assiduously avoiding the office chitchat that gobbles up time (but also sometimes greases the social wheels of promotion). You've likely learned how to beat back email creep and batch your work tasks so that you can operate as close to robotic efficiency as humanly possible. And you've probably even outsourced as much personal administrative and household stuff as you can afford to—Instacart, anyone?

Sometimes there's just way too freakin' much to do in too little time, regardless of all the "hacks" you incorporate into your routine (I promise not to say *hacks* again).

The only way to make room for the good stuff is to get rid of something not-so-good.

Starting our space-making journey with our physical space is important because it's a tangible way to chalk up a few wins and begin to
gain momentum. Sometimes when we go through old books, papers,
and memorabilia, we are reminded of old passions, and the process
even serves to rekindle some long-dormant ones that may want to
resurface. Marie Kondo also has a point about how clearing out the
stuff we no longer need primes our minds to release what they no
longer need and make room for what they do.

While I am confident that decluttering your home and/or office will
feel gratifying—liberating, even—I can't promise it will be easy or
pain free. We attach a lot of meaning and personal history to our
belongings, and moving through a process of evaluating them and
deciding for each one which should stay and go stirs up a lot of
emotional jetsam, inviting us to float with it a little while so we can
decide what works best for us now, and then release what we need to
release wholeheartedly, when we are ready. If your schedule is too full
to tackle the whole house now, don't worry. Even doing your desk, a
closet, or your clothing will offer you significant mind-decluttering
benefits and a sense of accomplishment and satisfaction. Pick one
spot and start there.

THE METHOD FOR MAKING PHYSICAL SPACE

Step 1

Try to set aside enough time to do a whole section at once, like a
closet or even a shelf of a closet. Let's say you are doing your linen
closet on a rainy Saturday morning. You simply pick up each item one
at a time and ask if it sparks joy. When I did this process, I also asked
if it was just plain useful, like towels, since although those aren't a
source of joy for me, we need them.

When doing the usefulness test, it's important to keep in mind *when*
an item will be useful. If it's useful now or during the next calendar
year (like winter clothes), keep them. If the answer is "someday"—for

things like all those hotel-sized soaps and lotions you've been collecting for the last 10 years—then let them go.

Step 2

Items with a *yes* are kept, and items with a *no* are thanked for their service and moved to the discard or donate piles. There's a humane society thrift shop near us, and we love donating stuff there since all the money goes to help abandoned animals. If you have enough clothes in good shape, you could ship them to ThredUp and sell them, using the credit you earn to enliven your wardrobe with some fresh, gently used fashion at no cost, and you get to be an eco-warrior to boot!

Try not to make a third "maybe" pile; this just delays the inevitable reckoning and makes the process more arduous. If you're attached to something, you can consider making the effort to try to find it a specific home among family or friends, but don't stress about this. There are lots of places and people out there that can make good use of your gently used items. Then you organize what you've decided to keep and give it a permanent place in the house (not just another pile or closet or box labeled "misc."). Keep it simple, and use items such as shoe boxes or other containers you may have already.

That's the basics!

Here are a few more considerations to keep in mind:

1. **Items like gifts that were given with care but are not particularly liked or useful can be tough to let go of, since we can confuse rejecting the item with rejecting the person.** Kondo assures us, though, that the items will be much happier in a home with someone who will love and use them. We can still hold gratitude in our hearts for the person who gifted us the item and be thankful for their investment of time, energy, and money in us.

2. **Don't spend hundreds of dollars at the Container Store to find ever-more-clever ways to stylishly store more than you need or want.** If your home truly has no shelving or closets, maybe find a useful piece of storage furniture, but don't even think about that until you've removed everything that doesn't pass the tests of joy and usefulness. Only put things away after you're sure they belong in your house.

3. **Consider implementing the *one in, one out* rule.** My family has always lived in homes without lots of bedroom closet space, and I've come to think of this as a good thing. We don't add a new piece of clothing or footwear unless we remove one. There's no room for both new and old, and it keeps the purging small and regular to help us avoid collecting too much and getting overwhelmed.

4. **Become a master at giving stuff away.** A few years ago, I had the idea that I was going to open a retail shop with plants, cute home goods, and tasty snacks. This idea lasted as long as one pop-up holiday shopping event, which I made my son staff with me. I quickly realized this was not actually going to work. I held a fundraiser for my favorite youth organization at my house later that year and raffled off the unsold retail stock items. We raised a bunch of money to send kids to summer camp, and all the boxes disappeared from my office. Perfect.

5. **Depending on your time and finances, you can call in reinforcements.** A client of mine hired a professional organizer to help overhaul her pantry. She had little time or interest in tackling this long overdue project and was thrilled with the outcome.

6. **Only purge your own stuff!** Another client needed to clear her office of her partner's extensive magazine collection. Since one of the decluttering rules is that it's personal, we can't dump other people's stuff without their consent, the client worked with her partner to sort and relocate the ones he really wanted to keep, found a storage location for them

outside of her office, and helped him let the others go. It was a difficult conversation and a process they'd been putting off for a while, so thoughtfully working though it was healing for both of them.

7. **Comedian George Carlin has a famous bit where he says: "A house is just a place to keep your stuff while you go out and get more stuff."** Of course, he takes this to its logical extreme, but it's very funny and eye opening in the process.

TAKE WHAT WORKS AND LEAVE THE REST

The KonMari Method also includes specific tips on folding clothes and organizing in general. Check out the book or show if you want the details on this. For most working folks, these will seem super fussy and tough to manage. While still on my break from work, I tried the folding, color-coding, and organizing tactics for my clothes. My drawers looked ah-mazing. Everything was folded and stacked so beautifully that I could select the perfect pair of socks that I truly wanted to wear each day with the birds chirping around my head just like in Cinderella (instead of throwing them all on the floor and frantically searching for a matching set).

Once back at work though, I went right back to my old laundry ways, which I call the "sort and stuff" method. I don't think this method is going to launch any TV shows, but for a working parent, it's magic and probably the only way my or my young children's clothing would ever actually see the inside of a drawer. I suspect you do some version of this too. Laundry piles get sorted into shirts, pajamas, etc. Once in piles, I stuff them into their respective drawers, push them closed, and voila, I can hit the sack in my now laundry-free bed. Periodically I'll do a drawer purge and part with the items crumpled in back that were never missed.

Now that they are older, my kids are on their own with their laundry. My son is 100 percent a sort-and-stuffer, and my daughter is kind of a hybrid case. They do an annual purge as well to remove things they've outgrown or no longer like, with a bit of support from me.

I hear now that Marie has kids of her own, she has ditched some of the more precious and time-consuming tasks, and I confess I do feel a sense of validation. Aha! It *was* impossible to do all this! Like working parents and other mere mortals, she's come to the realization that we can only do so much in a day. If given the choice between perfect drawers and more time to snuggle and read books with my kids or sip a nightcap with the hubs by the fire, the joy and connection that comes from snuggling and sipping wins every time.

But even though some techniques didn't stick, the basic teachings and benefits of freeing yourself of the burden of too much stuff is solid advice and it works.

The decluttered house was a dream and lasted several years before I had to do a refresher course. Having less stuff everywhere means less stuff to clean and organize—a gift that keeps on giving. The effects of purging are real and lasting, and well worth the effort.

BTW—I did keep the hanging items in the closet in rainbow order, since it takes no more time to hang stuff here or there, and that legit does bring me joy.

SWEDISH DEATH CLEANING

One of my clients who was a soon-to-be empty nester said she was contemplating doing a "Swedish Death Cleaning" session. Apparently, like Marie Kondo's method, this approach also has its own show! It involves organizing and decluttering your home before you die to lessen the burden on your loved ones.

The premise of Margareta Magnusson's book *The Gentle Art of Swedish Death Cleaning: How to Free Yourself and Your Family from a Lifetime of Clutter* involves the somewhat morbid but oh-so-true reminder that we can't take anything with us when we die, and that our best use of time here on earth is enjoying the present with those we care about, doing things that matter to us.

In concept, it's simple, and as long as we surround ourselves with only the useful and meaningful items in our lives, we're on the right track not only for our own happiness, but also for the future ease and joy of our loved ones.

I can definitely get behind this. I know our teenagers want very little of our stuff, and the last thing they will want to do after we die is deal with the things we've collected over the years. When my dad died, I can confidently say that he was *not* a Swedish death cleaning guy. In fact, I think he was prepping for the apocalypse. There were hundreds of cans of expired tomato sauce and other goods, a full-size log splitter (he was not a lumberjack), enough guns and ammo for a local uprising, and enough books and cookware to please Julia Child. Who needs eleven ceramic pie pans? My dad, that's who. As one of my brothers, who is both the executor and beneficiary and is still managing the mess, said: "It's the gift that keeps on taking."

THE BOTTOM LINE

Making physical space is the first step in climbing out of the trap so many of us fall into in the exhausting hustle and grind and the effort to "keep up with the Joneses"—and the burnout that results when we allow society's definition of success to override our own. Spending our time, energy, and money buying and dealing with mountains of stuff that will break, go out of style, and turn into clutter can keep us stuck and hold us back. Releasing the things that do not spark joy to support our journey now sets us free and is the first step toward reclaiming our well-being.

REFLECTION ACTIVITIES

Your turn to declutter!

- Choose a spot to tidy and a day and time to do it.
- Follow the steps above.
- Decide how you will nurture yourself after this. Decluttering can be quite a taxing process, and you'll want to plan to care for yourself after with rest or celebration or both.

Note how much lighter you feel after. Allow fresh thoughts and ideas to present themselves and when they do, note them! Gently get into the habit of noticing the ways your mind offers ideas and inspiration to you.

MAKE MENTAL SPACE

Relax, allow the mind to become empty, and surprise yourself with the great treasure that begins to flow from your soul.
— Paulo Coelho, *The Valkyries*

After I experienced the life-changing magic of tidying my house, I turned my sights on our front yard—also known as "the barren wasteland." Our front yard was the worst in the neighborhood, and probably not even inviting for dogs to do their business on it. We barely had time to do the must-do-to-live stuff on our list, and landscaping was so far down we forgot about it altogether. On the flip side, we could claim that the barren wasteland was evidence of us engaging in extreme water saving measures as truly excellent humans since we were in such a long and withering drought in California. Between you and me though, I'd rather have the *Sunset* magazine garden than title of Best Drought Survivor any day.

The literal house was in order, but my inner house still needed work, and I knew I needed to get grounded back into my body, mind, soul, and intuition. Redoing both front and back yards, by hand and on my own, seemed like a good place to start. It was a literal re-grounding that I knew would also help do some much-needed inner work.

Each morning I'd get the kids off to school, put on my overalls and boots, grab my pickaxe, and hack away at the concrete-like clay soil to loosen it, remove weeds, and finally mix in better soil. At the end of each day, I was covered in dirt and sweat, my hands swollen and blistered. I was getting stronger though, and the physical exhaustion was oddly relaxing compared to the chronic mental overload I'd grown accustomed to. It allowed me to sleep more soundly and to release some of the pent-up stress I'd unwittingly been carrying in my body for years.

Neighbors walking by were encouraging, and after a couple months of prep, the time finally came to choose and plant the newest additions to our garden. My kids came to the garden store and helped pick out the plants; we had a ball, and the yard looked amazing.

It was a grounding process indeed, and there's something very meditative about doing physical work. It requires focus yet allows the mind some space to creatively wander.

My mind didn't obsess or ruminate. Instead, it was allowed to lightly bounce around, letting new ideas bubble up and be seen, creating headspace through mindful action.

I even installed raised beds in the backyard so we could grow our own food and live off the land—a victory garden of sorts to symbolize my return to vitality. But anyone who actually farms will know very well that this is much harder than it looks. The stumpy little carrots, buggy strawberries, and seven cherry tomatoes we grew the first year were not exactly a bumper crop.

One more hot tip: Do not, under any circumstances, be persuaded to buy a bag of ladybugs on the internet to combat your aphid problem. I did, and I can assure you that within thirty seconds of you ceremoniously releasing them into the gourmet meal of your garden, they will use their beautiful little wings and fly far away, never to be seen again. All of them. Without eating even one of your terrible, horrible aphids.

Still, the process of making something lovely with my own hands where nothing once existed was gratifying and centering. Making space in our minds is essential if we want to live according to what matters most to us. In fact, we become almost like amnesiacs if we don't make this space. We lose touch with our inner knowing, what we really need and want, and fall into a sleeplike trance, doing all the things we think folks in our roles in life do while forgetting it's our job to write the screenplay of our lives, not just act them out.

NOURISHING OURSELVES IS AN INSIDE JOB

For many years on my road to burnout and during the digging-out process, I was convinced the problem was outside myself, and if I could just identify it, I'd be fixed. As part of this investigative process, however, I learned much about myself and about the truths of burnout. This section focuses on the fixes I tried—some while still working full time and other during my sabbatical break—and gives some notes on what I learned from each.

Functional Medicine

I was convinced I had some hard-to-diagnose medical ailment and put my considerable research skills to work googling every possible problem that matched my various symptoms. Surely my symptoms would align with one. I thought a functional medicine doctor would connect my mind and body together in a more holistic manner. Like many people, I found I had some things to check into, but oddly to my dismay, nothing too significant was uncovered. I needed to do a better job of eating well (no surprise), exercising more (like most of us), and managing my stress (like all of us). This goes without saying, but the doctor is an excellent first stop for a physical, bloodwork, and whatever else makes sense to rule out serious issues and follow up on things that warrant it.

Cognitive Behavioral Therapy (CBT)

This form of therapy is extremely useful in reframing a number of cognitive distortions that commonly take root in chronically stressed people. It provides a logical framework and strategy for getting out of your own head and for those of us that need to know the why and how of everything, it's quite enlightening. You can search for therapists who specialize in this method or if you want to find out more about how it works first, check out David D. Burns, M.D.'s excellent book *The Feeling Good Handbook*.

Mindfulness-Based Stress Reduction (MBSR)

One thing that moved the needle for me was taking an eight-week MBSR class in my area. These programs are all over the place and even online, and they're based on the work of Jon Kabat-Zinn and his book *Full Catastrophe Living*, which you can explore to do this program yourself.

Initially, I hid that I was doing this from colleagues at work because I didn't want to be seen as "weak," like I couldn't handle the pressure. But people noticed a positive difference in me and asked what had changed. I told them about the class, and some checked it out for themselves.

A year later, I was somewhat embarrassed to already need a tune-up on the practices we learned and took it again, but whatever; do what you have to do, and don't make it worse by judging yourself about it. It took decades to establish the neural pathways I had and would take time to reroute them to engage in healthier ways of managing stress and turmoil.

In the years since I did this, our society has come so far when it comes to talking about mental health and what it takes to truly care for ourselves and each other. Many people are faced with more stressors than they can comfortably cope with and more responsibilities than there are hours in the day. Learning how to manage our stress is an essential skill for living a rich, connected life.

A Spiritual Practice: Mindfulness, Meditation, Prayer

Many folks say, "I can't meditate" or "I'm bad at it." Both statements are impossible, as meditation and mindfulness aren't skills to be good or bad at. I used to think it was all about clearing my mind to be as empty and limitless as the sky on a bluebird day. Wrong. That's not possible either—for most people, anyway.

These are simply practices we cultivate over time, which allow us to be with things as they are, without getting into a fistfight with every thought or emotion that goes through our busy mind. It's literally a practice of not reacting so we have the presence of mind to respond thoughtfully or to simply let things go, depending on the situation. Want to learn to relax, listen to others, handle challenges, reduce stress, process feelings, be yourself, or be there for others? A mindfulness practice will support all of these.

One of the first mindfulness practices I learned was in the MBSR class: the "body scan." This is profoundly relaxing and centering, takes about ten minutes, and is easy to do. You can google a guided recording to follow or find one on the various mindfulness apps. Essentially, you lay flat on your back in as much ease as your body can muster. Take a few deep breaths and center your attention within your body.

Starting with your head and ending with your feet, focus your attention on one section of your body at a time, imagining you are breathing into and out of it, and gently acknowledging (but not thinking about or analyzing) any sensations you notice there. Doing this in the mornings before you start your day or as a way to wrap up before heading to bed is a lovely way to center and ground yourself within your body and mind so the information they have to share with you is more readily accessible.

If you were raised with prayer, do it anytime, anywhere, and in any form that feels good and natural to you. I got out of the habit of this for many years after having been raised doing it, and reconnecting with it has been a gift. It is centering, comforting, and restorative to simply talk with God and give over control of things I have no business trying to control anyway.

My sister and I recently went to visit a few tiny Greek islands and were delighted to find tiny churches big enough to hold just a few people at a time, open each evening for anyone to stop in and quietly reflect or light a candle and offer a prayer. Simple, direct, and regular connection to whatever our higher power is feels grounding and healing. And in today's busy, fraught, and sometimes overwhelming world, it feels especially important.

One final word on this. As we've noted here, mindfulness can take many forms—it is not just sitting on the floor attempting complete stillness. It can also look like regular life. A few ways I practice mindfulness while simply living are walking, running, swimming, and playing guitar. The physical activities invite presence by virtue of the mind-body connection they require. The guitar is sufficiently difficult that I must pay close attention, and this focus means that my brain can't go off on worry tangents at the same time. Plus, music is just a soul-soothing human gift.

Medications

For years I resisted trying even the smallest doses of anything that could help, from brain chemistry meds to even migraine prescriptions. Instead, I suffered needlessly and terribly, robbed of entire days of life under the vise of migraines, stressed well beyond my capacity to cope, scared of the side effects, and thinking I should not need this kind of support. Why couldn't I just *will* myself to get my shit together?!

When I had a full-blown panic attack at an evening networking event and had to hide in the storeroom for a while and call my sister,

Natalie, to settle down, I decided it was time to give medication serious consideration.

Over the years I've tried various forms of medication and adjusted as needed, and sometimes I've not needed anything at all. As far as I'm concerned now, we ought to use whatever useful and restorative tools we can to help navigate life's challenges, lessons, and legacies.

Essential Oils and Aromatherapy

I love good-smelling things and burn candles in our house like it's my job, but if you're far down the hole of exhaustion, overload, and anxiety, this option is not going to solve your problems—no matter what the nice lady on Instagram says. Do what you need to create a comfortable and relaxing vibe in your environment, as part of your overall approach to living well. It's not a magic fix, but it will support your overall mood and level of comfort, and that's never a bad thing.

Infrared Sauna

This is a contraption that uses light waves to heat the body rather than heating the air. Proponents say this means you can stay longer and sweat more. The brand Sunlighten is well regarded and has lots of information on these kinds of saunas. Health organizations like the Mayo Clinic have weighed in, saying they have been shown to provide some benefit as well. Infrared saunas are not going to single-handedly deliver you to perfect health, but I do enjoy it and have realized many of the benefits of sweating that it promises: relaxation, pain reduction, and happier skin.

Tapping (EFT)

EFT means Emotional Freedom Technique and is also called Tapping or Psychological Acupressure. Like acupuncture, it focuses on meridian points (energy points) in your body and seeks to balance them and restore flow, thus easing tension, stress, and mental or emotional blocks.

This approach was not useful to me when I first tried it, but I've since incorporated the practice into my routine from time to time at the urging of an excellent coach I worked with. I have found it useful for moving past certain negative thought patterns. It's kind of woo-woo for many people, but it's worth a try, as there are no harmful side effects and the guided videos online are free.

Acupuncture

Acupuncture uses thin needles to stimulate the nervous system and balance energy flow in the body. Many people use it for help with pain management, to ease allergies, anxiety, and stress, and to support healing from many other conditions.

This is not my favorite support option since I'm a wimp about needles, but my husband and friends swear by it. And the needles are really thin, so you can hardly feel them. I didn't stick with it long enough to form a personal opinion, but it's a low-risk (and in a group setting, affordable) option to try.

Yoga/Kickboxing

Every few years I try to take up yoga, and each time I think "Man, this is not for me." I used to joke that I wasn't mature enough for it. Maybe that's true. But, boy, could I use it, as I'm one of earth's least flexible humans. I know so many people who love it and find it very nourishing, so by all means, do what works best for you.

I'm more a kickboxing or Krav Maga gal, and if I ever take a movement class, those are the ones I lean into. Although not often considered "wellness" pursuits, I've gained a lot of good from them over the years. They teach both a strong body and a strong mindset—not of violence, but of a willingness to work with fear and confidence that you can manage whatever comes your way.

Exercise(!)

Okay, this one is as close to a magic pill or silver bullet as it gets. As basic and boring as it sounds and as essential as our doctors say it is when it comes to building a healthy body and mind, exercise is, well, the literal one thing to get into your schedule even if you do nothing else whatsoever. Even thirty minutes of exercise a day offers significant improvements to pretty much all areas of our well-being, including physical health, mental health, and sleep.

It's also the most fruitful thing I do in terms of opening the floodgates for creative problem solving and coaxing fresh ideas to emerge. I'm always pausing in order to capture an idea that comes to me in the notes app on my phone. If you're a phone-free exerciser, carry a scrap of paper and a tiny pen. You'll need it.

Exercise is relatively quick, cheap, and—once you make it into a habit—easy to maintain. I axed movement (swimming, running, kickboxing, even walking) from my life for years due to being overbooked and overwhelmed and in the attempt to get everything else done first.

That turned out to be a very bad idea, and it took me a good long while to reestablish this as a reliable part of my life. But oh my God is it worth it. Seriously. Just move most days in any way you can, outside, if possible. I swear by this one and if it doesn't help you after thirty days of doing it, I'll buy you a drink.

Ayahuasca. Just kidding. Too scared to try this but had to add it as the accounts I've read and seen of people doing it are pretty fascinating. One of these days I may try it and will report back.

Final Thoughts

If I had to boil my "tour for the cure" above into one lesson, it would be this: Our health and well-being require our diligent care and attention. Some of the remedies and practices I tried helped a lot, and some not so much. There was no specific aliment causing all my problems that I could identify, excise, and move on from. I needed to make some systemic changes in how I was thinking about and using my time, energy, and resources.

Many of the practices I learned became ingredients in my recipe for well-being that works for me. But it was still up to me to make sure I prioritized these in my life and let go of the habits, actions, and beliefs getting in my way. All of this was in my power and control all along. I just had to learn how to care about my own well-being enough and incorporate the practical skills required.

LET'S TALK ABOUT LIMITING-BELIEF GREMLINS

Limiting beliefs are nasty gremlins. Watch out for their evil ways. Just like the gremlins in the movie that gave us all nightmares as kids, they seem friendly and benign enough at first, when they are little Mogwai —but if you don't manage them well, all hell breaks loose. They make us say *no* to ourselves, often for no good reason.

These inaccurate beliefs get planted in all sorts of ways without us even noticing if we aren't careful.

The dean of students at my high school once pulled me aside to inform me I was not as smart or capable as I thought I was. He questioned why I was bothering to even try to do all the various academic and extracurricular activities I was involved in since it would get me nowhere and I couldn't handle it all anyway. The school had been all boys for 100 years, and I was among just a few girls admitted into the first coed class. He was hostile to the girls in a general way, and outright nasty to me. Apparently, he thought I needed to be knocked down a peg or ten.

A former boss once told me and anyone else who would listen that I was uncreative in the extreme, an opinion I took as fact for longer than I care to admit.

A former coworker who had seniority compared to me (but was not my boss or performing the same scope of work) said my chief virtue was insubordination and complained about me, simply because I declined to do things the way he thought they should be done. He thought he knew my job better than I did and hated that I wouldn't comply with his meddling.

I'm sure folks in positions of authority or seniority over you have abused their roles as well in ways large and small, trying to cram you into a teeny tiny box of their own making; no one is immune. When people (especially parents, teachers, bosses, and others whose opinions we are taught to regard) don't believe in us, it can cause us to question our belief in ourselves.

Unfortunately, people say random shit all the time, and 99 percent of the time, it's a reflection of what's going on with them and has very little to do with you. Like a gremlin that gets wet and multiplies, input from the dominant culture, marketing and advertising, terrible teachers or coaches, and unskillful or just plain abusive family, friends, bosses, and coworkers festers and grows when we believe it and offer it our energy and headspace. Over time, these can grow into a very nasty inner critic that we turn on ourselves.

Awareness and inquiry are like sunlight to these inner gremlins: They kill them.

It's useful to look clearly in the light of day at the fact-free proclamations of our inner jerk. Noticing uncharitable assumptions and asking ourselves what information we have to support the belief goes a long way toward defanging this beast.

Some of my favorite questions to ask myself when one rears its ugly head include: Is this true? How do I know? What information supports this? What else could be true? What facts support that? Where did this idea even come from? What benefit do I get from continuing with these self-defeating thoughts and playing small?

Perhaps some sort of protection from external criticism? What benefit might I get from releasing them?

The next time you find yourself spinning out and acting like your own worst enemy, take a time-out. Shine a light on the tornado of shit swirling in your head, remember who TF you are; remember all the times you persevered through challenges, the things you learned, and that at the core you are a capable, powerful, worthy human. What would this grounded and confident version of you say or do in this situation? That's self-possession, and it's your golden ticket.

REFLECTION ACTIVITIES

- What activity might you do to help yourself create some mental space?
- When will you do this and for how long?
- What supportive practices might you investigate and experiment with?
- What self-imposed boundaries or limiting belief gremlins might be lurking beneath the surface? Take a look at them in the light of day and see if you can shift your thinking and be more supportive of yourself, your humanity, the fact that we're all learning and growing, and that most of what others say and do has nothing to do with us.

Here's another strategy for making mental space. I did this with my kids, and I now share it with clients, and it's called "glitter breathing." Some folks are more into mindfulness exercises than others. Some of my clients say the notion of it is rage inducing. For them, and everyone really, try this instead. I prefer to call it glitter breathing anyway, because it seems more fun and frankly is quite an accurate description of what it is.

Start with an old glass jar with a lid. Rinse thoroughly and remove the label. Put in a tablespoon or two of your favorite glitter color(s). Fill the rest with water and put on the lid. Shake liberally and watch the jar until all the glitter settles. Take deep breaths while watching and imagine your thoughts settling with each breath just like the glitter settles.

As your breathing settles, your thoughts will settle too, and at the end, you'll have done a couple minutes of relaxing deep breathing and calmed your nervous system. Keep it at your desk or wherever you like and repeat as needed.

MAKE SPACE IN YOUR SCHEDULE AND SET BOUNDARIES

If I didn't define myself for myself, I would be crunched into other people's fantasies for me and eaten alive.
— Audre Lorde

Often the people who get most burned out are the ones who get it done in life and work, no matter what. They find that extra gear even through bone-deep exhaustion, when they didn't even know that gear existed. They are reliable to the core. They are the kind of team players who know sometimes the demands are higher and that's how it goes, so we may have to grind for a bit. They stick it out day and night when things are hard with family life and often put up with unhealthy amounts of BS from others in their lives.

Sound like you? Then you're also the kind of person who takes pride in your work and does it well, even when no one is breathing down your neck (maybe *especially* when no one is breathing down your neck). You take pride in the quality of your work and the mission it serves and try hard to treat others well and build meaningful relationships along the way. You're a dream team member.

Unfortunately, high performers like this often keep pressing on, year after year, proving that we can crush everything thrown at us, all while silently dying inside waiting for someone to turn down the volume, throw us a life preserver, and just go away. And we keep doing it until something literally collapses, breaks, or otherwise snaps us to attention in the form of an emergency or health crisis. Any person (even any mechanical thing) that keeps going without time to recharge (or undergo maintenance) eventually breaks down. It's inevitable, and it's magical thinking to believe otherwise.

This is what I refer to with my clients as the "efficiency tax."

The efficiency tax is the lovely "reward" high performers get when they consistently go above and beyond, taking on more and more until external demands have replaced every "free" hour on their schedule at work and in their personal lives. Doing everything for everyone else until every trace of time with family and friends, walking outdoors, at painting class, playing piano, doing tai chi, sitting on the beach, sleeping (you get the point) has been removed in hopes of finally reaching the bottom of the bottomless to-do list and ensuring no one is let down or inconvenienced.

When folks around us see that we are still getting it all done (or we seem to be on the outside, at least), they think we have capacity and keep piling more on. Instead of winning an all-expenses-paid vacation to a tropical island, we "win" (and have unwittingly trained others to give us) more tasks to do.

This is true even when we are saying verbally that the status quo is not sustainable. Our actions (of getting it all done) speak louder than our words and sometimes managers simply hope that our fatigue has simply "gone away" after a three-day weekend spent lying in bed with a skull-crushing migraine and pillow over our head. Didn't we get *enough rest* already? (No.)

When the ever-increasing demands from others devour the things we need to build a solid foundation of mental, physical, and spiritual well-being, we become unmoored, unbalanced, and un-fun. Exhaustion spikes, resilience wanes, and we lose track of the pathway back to the life we want to live.

Often what happens next is that we get pissed off at others, blaming them for our being overwhelmed when we're the ones who didn't set boundaries or clearly install protective fencing around our time in the first place.

Blaming ourselves is equally unhelpful. After all, most of us got here in the first place by attempting to satisfy the spoken or unspoken work and societal expectations, gritting our teeth and grinding it out, never missing a beat and never revealing the mess under the surface.

It's more about reminding ourselves that we hold the power (and the responsibility) to protect and spend our time according to the dictates of our own inner compass, and we give that power away by allowing others (sometimes very pushy others) to overfill our schedules, and then blaming them for doing so.

Sadly, time is a zero-sum game. We only get twenty-four hours each day, and it's up to us to spend them as well as we can on the people and things that matter most in our lives—while making a living in the process and modeling to others through our own acts of self-regard that we are worthy of respect.

Though we often think of things like rest, exercise, time with loved ones, and doing things that light us up as "extras," to be done "if there's extra time" (which there never is), they are in fact essential. They belong at the top of our to-do list, rooted literally and firmly on our schedules, as immutable as gravity.

When we regularly overwrite our weekly fitness class with another "urgent" demand, we fail to keep our commitments to ourselves. As painful as it is to admit, *we* are the ones who allowed this to occur. But the excellent news is that we are also the ones with the ability to change it and to practice treating ourselves and our time with greater care and respect in the process.

WHERE DOES THE RUBBER MEET THE ROAD? YOUR SCHEDULE

Let's talk about your schedule, the way you allocate your time *and* energy. Both of which, sadly, are finite resources—the fossil fuels of human life. But by intentionally choosing which people and things make it onto our schedules and mental radar, we can tap into our natural renewable resources: joy and love.

We can have all the amazing ideas in the world for how we want to live and what we want to do. But until we make space and time for those things, they will continue to be ideas on Post-its at our desk or fleeting longings in our mind, set aside for "someday" when we magically have more time and focus than we do today. Except that day doesn't come uninvitedly.

We must decide if it's important enough to invite it in and make it happen.

This chapter is all about identifying and implementing practical strategies for prioritizing your well-being in a world that would prefer you conform, play the status and consumption game, and take care of everyone and everything else first.

ENERGY AUDIT AND REALLOCATION

We function best when we do things that feed our energy instead of depleting it. Seems obvious, but unless we are intentional about this, we are just buckets full of holes, with energy pouring out all over the place toward whatever pulls the hardest or is easiest to mind-numbingly slip into. Doing energy-giving activities leaves us primed for even more love and adventure in our lives, and more to give to those who matter most. Doing energy-depleting activities has the opposite effect.

Why not feed the one that feeds us back?

Here's an energy audit exercise for you. You'll need a piece of paper, pen, and colored highlighters.

- Make two lists: one of everything you do on a typical weekday and one of everything you do on a typical weekend day.
- Circle the stuff that is 100 percent required to be done by you to ensure your survival and that of your dependents. Really ask if each one has to be done *that way, by you,* in order to *survive* rather than to be comfy in the status quo, or the exact same lifestyle to which you've become accustomed.
- This is also a good time to consider the degree to which all members of your household (partners, roommates, and children) are contributing appropriately to domestic activities. This is a can of worms on its own I realize. These will be deemed essential, and we're not going to tackle these right now; we're going to leave them alone.
- For all the stuff not circled, we'll deem these nonessential for the purposes of this exercise. For these:
- Use a green or blue highlighter to mark the activities that give you energy. These could also elicit feelings of relaxation, well-being, joy, or fun.

- Use a pink or orange highlighter to mark the ones that take energy. These leave you feeling tired, depleted, or like you need to crawl under a rock to hide for a while.
- Ask yourself which of the nonessential items you can remove from your typical weekday and your typical weekend day. What could you replace them with? More of something from the energy-giving list? More sleep? Exercise? Something new and exciting from your "maybe I'll get to this someday" list?

WORK CREEP

We're all familiar with the concept "work creep" and the way it tends to gobble up every ounce of time and energy we have, regardless of how wonderful our energy maximizing efforts are. It's rooted in the old and hard-to-kill work-life balance paradigm we talked about earlier, which assumes paid work is the top (and at times, the only) priority. It feels like for every hour we liberate on our schedule, work is there to eagerly fill the time. Even in the old days this was true, but nowadays it's even harder to set healthy boundaries on it and create life-work balance, where work is but a part of the ecosystem of our lives.

Here's why.

At some point in the early 2000s, many of us became equipped with enough technology to work from anywhere—wow! And boy, we did. Except instead of working from the beach, we just came home from work, spent some time with our families (eating, doing nighttime routines, cuddling with books and songs, and chores), only to crack open that email or an ongoing project and work some more. How flexible, we thought. Except for many of us, this flexibility was a one-way street.

We gave more of our personal time to work, and work did not give any of its traditional time (eight a.m. to six p.m. or whatever the official hours were) back to us. If we were really committed, we thought, we'd respond to that email from the boss at one a.m. and ensure that clients never waited a moment to receive a response to their needs. Now work was happening all the time, seven days a week in some cases, at all hours of the day. And at some companies, this willingness to be on the clock 24/7 was rewarded with pay and titles, even if the resultant work product was not higher or better than others who did not embrace this always-on mentality of work. In many cases, the work product was lower since it's easy for things to take forever when you apparently have forever, and work done by burned-out zombies is not particularly thoughtful, innovative, or excellent.

I tried to play this game for a little while, competing with the men in my office and broader industry who either had no caregiving responsibilities or had stay-at-home wives managing their home life and children in all ways. Predictably, it was a disaster. My already-taxed body and brain grew more and more brittle, and those most important to me received an exhausted and unpleasant me at the end of the day.

I added in more time away (actually using my paid time off without working the whole time) and put in some boundaries around work availability, but these Band-Aids were too little too late. I eventually cracked, so badly burned out that I had to leave the grind completely in order to recover.

LIFE-WORK BALANCE IN PRACTICE

Toward the end of my sabbatical break, I'd restored myself to the point where I was actually excited to get back into work and was amazed at the ideas and energy that had been restored. I interviewed with several firms in my field of housing development and found that the expectations of 100 percent commitment to work were alive and well in all of them, maybe even worse than when I'd left nearly two years earlier. But I was excellent at what I did and was determined to find a way to do it that wouldn't plunge me right back into the pit of burning hell I'd just spent all this time climbing out of.

I decided to open a consulting business in my field and look for clients with interesting projects who needed support from a seasoned veteran like me. I ended up working for several years with terrific clients on exciting projects and had developed the skills and experience to set up our working relationship in a sustainable manner. They knew I was invested in their success and would take exceptional care of the work and team entrusted to my leadership. I was available as needed for in-person work and performed the rest according to my schedule and availability, balancing various client needs with my own needs and those of my family.

I proved what I'd intuitively known all along: that hustle culture was a lie, and that it was absolutely possible to work with the values of excellence, purpose, and autonomy at the core.

And that in engaging in a solopreneur consulting capacity, I could make more money working fewer hours, finally being paid what my contributions were worth. Since I didn't allow myself to become oversubscribed, I had the energy and focus needed to lead my teams with care, creativity, and a clear head, and to be a much more present and fun human being for my family and friends.

The highest performers I know take setting boundaries and establishing healthy expectations for their life-work balance seriously. They care deeply about their work yet clearly understand paid work is but one element of a rich, multidimensional life. They nourish themselves, their relationships, and their passions.

For them, work is not primary, with everything else squeezing in around it where it can maybe sort of fit in. *Life* is primary, and the values, people, paid and unpaid work, and other interests they care about are given their due space and time within it.

I now help clients in all realms of work, from employee to solopreneur to entrepreneur create their own life-work balance so they can care for themselves and their lives while producing excellent work and paying the bills in the process. Sometimes they can make these adjustments within their current work environment, and sometimes they choose to find other opportunities, capacities, or pathways where they can establish a better fit and focus on mutual benefit with their work partners.

BOUNDARIES AND THE MAGIC OF THE WORD "NO"

Welcome to training day for learning how to say no to people and things that are not moving you closer to the life *you* actually want to live, closer to alignment with *your* gifts and values, or closer to what matters most to *you*. Without comfort and skill in this department, it's easy to be eaten up by this world and spat out in a pile of bones.

For many of us, this kind of boundary-setting feels inconceivable.

I can't tell you how many times I've suggested to a client that they simply decline an overreaching request/demand from work or personal life. And I get it. A therapist years ago made the heretical suggestion that I just say no and not do a bunch of unnecessary shit that people in my personal life wanted me to do, even though I was working full time (and not setting adequate boundaries there either!), raising kids, and had already cut out anything that could possibly be considered self-care or fun.

My upbringing suggested that one must always first see to the needs of others, especially elders. Even if our own needs were not being met and we lacked time and space for ourselves and the people and things *we* deemed most important. I think this was rooted in a mix of old-school Italian culture of obligation, Catholic Church, and the challenges of breaking unhealthy generational cycles in family life with varying degrees of success. I'd always had a fair bit of nerve (ask my coworker who described me as "insubordinate"), but for some reason while in a state of depleted burnout, I had trouble accessing that part of me and self-advocating while still feeling like I was a "decent" human being, which was important to me at the time. (It still is; I just don't define it by how pleased other people are with me.) I've also backed off on holding myself to impossibly high standards in all realms of life. Perfectionism of any kind just gets in the way.

I'm now far more concerned with being a happy, sane, self-possessed human, which is due both to personal growth and to simply getting older. One of the benefits of aging is caring so, so, so much less about what the rest of the world thinks of you, and also realizing they're not thinking all that much about you anyway! Growing into midlife and learning that we can't love or do honest, good deeds for others if we lack the ability to love, respect, and care for ourselves is a game-changer.

PRACTICAL STRATEGIES FOR SELF-POSSESSED BOUNDARY SETTING

What's the best way to decline an unwarranted encroachment on your schedule? The next time external pressure threatens the things we require to maintain our well-being, we can say simply that we have a conflict and can't accommodate the request. (Unless it's a true emergency, which 99.9 percent of the time it isn't.) We need not explain further what the "conflict" or "other commitment" is or defend our decision. It could be a class, a pedicure, a special afternoon date with your kids or partner, a walk in the park to decompress after receiving painful news, whatever.

Self-possessed self-care looks like taking time to care for the most important people and things in our lives, including ourselves. I've declined tons of requests over the last several years simply because I know I need down time, not necessarily because there was another event-level conflict in the way.

I don't ask permission because it is not theirs to give. It's my job to see to my well-being. Over time, folks will get used to our lack of 24/7 availability, and the pressure will fade. We'll also get used to prioritizing what we need to be true to show up fully and well in the world.

Here's a starter pack of ways to say "no" at work:

- "I wouldn't be able to give that project the time it needs and deserves, but let's see if we can find another solution."
- "Let's revisit priorities and see if we can fit it in. What project can wait or be reassigned to make space for this one?"
- "I'm afraid I'm at capacity and can't take that on."
- "I have a conflict/commitment at that time." (No one needs to know what these "commitments" are; they could be life- or work-related.)
- "I'm not available then, but here are a few times that would work." (Only use this if you truly plan to fit it in in the future.)
- "I know someone else who may be interested." (Use this if you do in fact know someone like this.)
- "I don't have the capacity to take on social event planning in addition to my core work responsibilities." (This one is for folks who get pushed into doing all the social glue stuff at work without pay, respect, or thanks. Sometimes doing this stuff is actually detrimental to your career, as it can lead to you not being seen as a leader but more like the "office mom.")
- "No, thank you."
- "No."

If you're laughing and laughing because you know that no one, ever, in the history of your organization, has ever even thought of establishing a work boundary due to the certain punishment or firing it would trigger, you have three options:

1. Say nothing and allow the status quo to continue, knowing this workplace has no respect for your life.
2. Try boundary-setting and test your assumption. The response from your coworkers might surprise you or it might not, but at least you'll know for sure and can decide how to respond accordingly.
3. Start talking with trusted family, friends, colleagues, or a coach about making a change and figure out a new direction.

Here are ways to say "no" to social or volunteer-type requests that you want to decline:

- "Sounds lovely, but my plate is full right now."
- "Thank you for the invite, but I can't join."
- "I have other plans that day but have a great time." (No one needs to know your other plans. They may involve binging Season 1 of *Bridgerton* in your pajamas with a plate of fried chicken, and that is a perfectly valid reason to decline their offer.)
- "Your organization does important work, but I can't take on additional volunteer opportunities at this time."
- "I appreciate you thinking of me, but I can't take on anything new at the moment."
- "I know someone else who may be interested." (Use only if you do in fact know someone like this.)
- "No, thank you."
- "No."

Notice the words "I'm sorry" are nowhere to be found on this list. Do *not* apologize for living. It's awkward for both you and them. Boundaries are healthy, necessary, and your responsibility to set, and there's nothing wrong and everything right with doing it.

Here's a little self-audit you can do to uncover why setting boundaries may be challenging:

- Do you feel the need to please others or make them happy?
- Do you think the well-being of other adults is your responsibility?
- Do you crave approval and acceptance from others?
- Do you fear rejection from others?
- Do you have trouble sharing how you really feel (such as disagreeing or declining to participate)?
- Do you feel trapped or taken advantage of in your work or personal relationships?
- Have you lost touch with how you feel about certain things in your pursuit of making others comfortable?

Each of these are indicators we are tying our self-worth to the opinions, feelings, actions, and approval of others, all of which are outside our control and ultimately irrelevant to our well-being. When we allow external circumstances and other people to dictate our thoughts, moods, and actions, we give our power away.

No shade, and don't stress. I've been there—and so have billions of other people. The great news is, we have the power to make healthy shifts in our lives and can start today. Remember that saying *no* to things that don't light us up makes room for us to say *yes* to things that do.

We can begin to recognize and accept that the only things we can really control are our *own* thoughts, actions, and habits. Our core value as a human being is intrinsic to us, and can never be granted by others, and thus never taken away.

Here's a practice you can start now, that will strengthen your self-worth muscle: Start keeping your word to yourself.

What does this mean?

It means treating "commitments" to yourself—exercise, sleep, practicing an instrument, a spiritual practice, lunch breaks, time with loved ones, days off—like they matter. Like *you* matter.

It means literally putting activities that contribute to your health, well-being, and happiness onto your calendar and then doing them at the appointed time. Guard the time allotted to them like gold, like it's an appointment with the president that would be rude to blow off.

You'll start giving off the confident vibe of someone who takes their own interests and needs seriously. Someone very grounded and capable. Someone who keeps commitments both to themselves and others. Someone you can trust. Someone you should also treat well, since they are worthy.

Put another way, others will never give us more time and respect than we give ourselves. In this way, we train others in how to treat us.

Cancelling on ourselves is an act of disrespect—poor treatment we would be loath to bestow on others—so why reserve the worst for ourselves? It's like eating the burned cookie because you don't want to give it to others. Okay, I get that, but why does anyone need to eat it? Just throw it out!

Before I learned to set healthy boundaries and truly prioritize my needs (which started with paying attention to and knowing what they even were), I would have these vivid fantasies of escape. Some would be sexy and glamourous, like picking up and moving to a foreign country with my family, living off the grid, never to look back. Some were kind of concerning in retrospect, like wishing to just disappear for a while and reappear when the apocalypse was over.

Funny story (in a sad way that will make you lose faith in humanity): A friend of mine is a kickass realtor and works her tail off to get the results her clients want. She got so burned out she was literally hospitalized, and guess what one of her clients said to her coworker (who was capably managing his needs in my friend's absence)? He demanded to speak to her about his "urgent" home sale question while she was *in the hospital.*

The nasty little moral of this story is that some folks will dish out as much crap as they think we'll take. They lack the self-regulation to know that just because you *can* possibly get away with certain behavior doesn't make it a great idea. We must, for the love of all that is good in this world, learn to meet our own needs and set boundaries and keep to them. No one is coming to save us.

Taking care of ourselves is our responsibility, and I promise you that once you start treating your time and yourself with respect, others will follow your example. You'll also be sufficiently clear-headed that you'll be able to choose the people in your life thoughtfully (and ditch the creeps who don't fit with your new regime of self-respect).

When we're clear on who we are and what we're worth, it becomes much easier to spot the people who don't give a shit about us and happily send them away, letting them carry their own baggage. You'll also have the energy and presence to show up so much more lovingly for the people and things that matter most.

THE BEST PART OF MAKING THIS SHIFT

In addition to being a hell of a lot more centered, present, and joyful, our work also benefits from being given guardrails and structure. When we are rested, energized, and whole, we bring a much deeper capacity for connection, focus, precision, innovation, and creative problem solving to the teams and projects we care so much about.

Contrary to what hustle culture tells us, healthy boundaries are a win-win proposition. With practice, you'll be a pro at setting them quicker than you think, and self-possession is not far behind.

REFLECTION ACTIVITIES

- Revisit the exercises and questions in this chapter. Any insights?
- What schedule changes can you make to ensure your time is being spent on what matters most?
- What promise can you keep to yourself?
- Identify an optional task you've been plugging along with that you really would rather not do. Practice saying no the next time it comes up.
- Think of a boundary you might want to establish and how you might announce it.
- Give yourself grace, credit, and a loving hug; this can be a scary and hard set of skills to practice.

REBUILDING: START WITH YOUR VISION

Energy flows where attention goes.
— Tony Robbins

When my daughter was young, before the burnout reached a fever pitch and the subsequent sabbatical break, we made a little art project on orange construction paper called our "future book." Mine had a number of things on it: long-term travel with my family, starting my own business, writing a book, learning to rock climb, paint, speak Spanish, and play guitar.

It was a simple list written in marker with some illustrations, doodles, and stickers, and I taped it to the bookcase near my bed so I saw it each morning and night. It was to be my first "vision board" of sorts, and just having it there meant some of my mental and emotional energy and imagination each day went toward those things, gradually filling in the details.

My son was born two years after my daughter, right into the recession that came after the financial collapse of 2007. There were mass layoffs, and my husband and I needed both our incomes to pay the mortgage on our (now underwater) house, support our kids, and help our parents. Given how limited our time and cash were, many of the things on the list felt very far out of reach—for a while, anyway.

Fast forward seven years or so, through various stages of burnout and work style adjustments, including dropping to four days a week for a year to give us time to plan financially for the much-needed leave from work, all the while living below our means so we could save as much money as possible and ultimately allow for more freedom of choice in our lives.

I was running on fumes that last year or so, and it took every ounce of grit I had to get to the finish line.

When given the time and effort needed to develop them, so many things that seemed impossible before became possible. As I worked through my self-compiled laundry list of books, classes, strategies, advice, and exercises—as I learned more and more about what I actually wanted and needed as well as what helped and worked—it was like the storm clouds parted and light shone through, illuminating ideas, possibilities, and pathways that had been invisible before.

Life seemed more saturated in color, and I regained the ability to be and have fun again, and to appreciate and nurture the unique sources of joy for others in my life. As of this writing, I've tried and experienced all of the things in my "future book" and have incorporated many into my everyday life.

EVERYTHING THAT BECOMES ANYTHING STARTS AS A SIMPLE THOUGHT

Let's start with some questions to get your imagination revved up:

- What do you most enjoy doing?

- Who do you enjoy spending time with?
- Who do you value most in your life?
- Where do you most like to go?
- If you could live anywhere, where would it be?
- If you could do anything for a living, what would it be?
- If you could create anything, what would it be?
- What are you naturally, magically good at (that you also enjoy)?
- What kinds of books do you read? What do you naturally enjoy learning about?
- What is your heart's desire?
- What do you truly want and wish for?
- What do you think you were meant to do on this earth?
- What do you value most in life? (Ideas include relationships with family and friends, adventure and exploration, curiosity, creativity, lifelong learning, purposeful leadership, service to others, cultivating excellence in a certain area, innovation, health and well-being.)

Many of us have had the wonder smashed out of us by the realities of adulthood, limiting beliefs of others and ourselves, conventional "wisdom," and the like, and we think of dreams as Disney-sparkle-castle-inspired BS. Because of our overly developed practicality muscle and human instinct for survival, we tend to reject out-of-hand the notion that we can begin to create a new future for ourselves beginning with a few simple ideas, or that we can (or deserve to) change much at all.

But doesn't everything start as a thought? Granted, most things end there too, but everything you've ever done started with an idea, a thought. Which thoughts bring you closer to where you want to go? Which turn into worry-fueled ruminations that get in the way of your connection with yourself and others, your fun and joy, and your development as a person? Realizing we can choose which thoughts we spend our time and energy on—and that the ones we nurture will grow—is a powerful start.

One of my clients in her 60s tried vision-boarding for the first time in my program called Sabbatical in a Box (which guides clients in a small group Zoom setting through much of what we are talking about in this book, from the comfort of home). She's a savvy and successful woman and was skeptical of the idea. She gave it a try anyway and came to love and see the value in it. She created a simple collection of words and a few images and put it on top of her dresser so she'd see it every morning.

Bit by bit, it started to shift the content of her waking thoughts and ideas of what was possible and helped her focus on what she really wanted.

She started to get more comfortable with the idea that what her intuition was telling her was important in her life *was* in fact important, that her dreams were possible, and that both were worth her attention, consideration, and energy.

In this chapter, we will explore visualization, how it works, and how you can incorporate it into cultivating your dream life. Time to visualize a new beginning. Let's go!

7 YEARS FROM NOW FEVER DREAM TIME MACHINE

Here again are the questions you reflected on a few moments ago.

- What do you most enjoy doing?
- Who do you enjoy spending time with?
- Who do you value most in your life?
- Where do you most like to go?
- If you could live anywhere, where would it be?
- If you could do anything for a living, what would it be?
- If you could create anything, what would it be?

- What are you naturally, magically good at (that you also enjoy)?
- What kinds of books do you read? What do you naturally enjoy learning about?
- What is your heart's desire?
- What do you truly want and wish for?
- What do you think you were meant to do on this earth?
- What do you value most in life? (Ideas include relationships with family and friends, adventure and exploration, curiosity, creativity, lifelong learning, purposeful leadership, service to others, cultivating excellence in a certain area, innovation, health and well-being.)

Once you have a response in mind for at least a few of them, you're ready to start the Fever Dream Time Machine activity below. You'll need a pen and paper or a computer. This should take you twenty to thirty minutes to complete, and you'll want a quiet, comfortable, uninterrupted space in which to do it.

- **Imagine** it's seven years into the future and write down everything you are doing in as much detail as you can. Engage all five senses as you do this: What does it look like, sound like, smell like, taste like, and feel like. The goal is to really immerse yourself into this process so deeply it almost feels real right now. What are you wearing, where are you living, who else is in your household, who is central in your life, are there new people, partners, friends there? What do you do for work, how much do you earn, have you retired from your current career, and what are you learning about now? What do you do for fun and recreation, what do you do for exercise, how do you get around? How is your home designed, and what does your furniture look like, what is the lighting like, what fragrances do you notice, what do you see out your windows, what kind of natural environment is nearby? How do you give to the community and the world? What is your health like, how do you care for yourself? Do you travel, and if so, how often and where? Do you have a spiritual practice, and what does it entail…?

- **Dream** big and do not censor or edit yourself in any way. Just keep going and writing down anything that comes into your stream of consciousness until nothing else comes out. Allow yourself the space and permission to sink into this, suspending judgment and your inner critic for the duration. It's okay if you find some of what has emerged to be surprising; we rarely allow ourselves to escape dull old practicality and conventional thinking and expectations. Allow yourself to feel excitement for the things that really resonate and openness that they can indeed become reality for you.

- **Create** something visual to represent the life you've imagined. Keep it as simple or elaborate as you feel like doing. The important thing is that you create *something* and then do the follow-through steps below. In my experience, when it comes to visualizing success, what works for different people varies. Some people swear by visual images like sketches, personal photos, or magazine clippings. Some respond better to words. Some like a combination.

VISUALIZING AS A PRACTICE

Some people may think vision board projects are bunk because it seems like a quick collage project; once complete, it goes into the closet and somehow does magic by itself from in there. I agree—that does sound like BS.

I've heard of the vision board being rebranded as an *action* board, which makes sense to me since without follow-up thoughts *and* the actions to support them, we're going nowhere fast.

Visualization is the act of creating compelling and vivid images and scenes in your mind. It's about vision and action combined—small investments of time and action, done consistently over time, usually months and sometimes years.

For five minutes a day, either first thing in the morning or before you go to bed, look at your vision board and use the Dos and Don'ts below to guide you. As you go about your day, incorporate related actions described below as well.

Do

- Visualize everything you imagined in rich, juicy detail.
- Feel the feelings associated with your desired outcomes being true right now. If you will feel happy and proud, then take time to feel those feelings now.
- Imagine your desired outcomes as already here and express gratitude for having them in your life.
- Allow seemingly random connections and ideas to emerge as part of this process and follow up on them.
- Remain open to your intuition and follow it in the direction of what lights you up.
- Do what you can, with what you have, and each day take the next "right" micro step that makes sense to you at the time.
- Keep learning and exploring and enjoying the process. Research, talk to others who know more about the things you're envisioning, enroll in a class, and allow this expanded store of knowledge and ideas help inform your next best step.
- Accept that not every move you make will yield quick or obvious results.
- Keep moving forward, believing in your ability to be creative, resourceful, resilient, and deserving of your heart's desire.

Don't

- Get caught up in every single detail of how any of this is going to come to fruition. Some goals have hundreds or thousands of steps to reach them, and it's impossible to plan it all in advance. Each step needs to interact with outside forces, and like a dancer you'll need to be flexible and adaptable after each move in order to make your next one.
- Cling to limited specifics with regard to the pathway you will take to get there. Be open to pivoting as new information is learned and new situations arise.
- Attach your ideal outcome to *specific* people in your personal life or at work. We can't control other people, and staying open to the wide variety of people in this world who might be open to exploring with us leaves us open to the widest array of possibilities and opportunities. The same goes for *specific* job titles or companies we may want to partner with; there are so many more options than we can possibly conceive of, and tunnel-visioning toward one or two makes us blind to the rest.

Revisit your time machine writing exercise and the vision board once per year, adding and adjusting details as you make progress.

Don't be afraid to change things as you move forward; it is natural that the process evolves as your dreams interact with the world, you receive feedback, and your experience evolves.

We start to claim responsibility for our lives by knowing the thoughts we cultivate and choose to focus on have power. We center our choices by prioritizing our well-being and the people and things that light us up. Visualizing is a powerful arrow in our quiver as we create the life of our dreams.

REFLECTION ACTIVITIES

Here's a quick summary of the Fever Dream Time Machine activity. Details above.

- **Grab** a pen and paper or a computer. This should take you twenty to thirty minutes to complete, and you'll want a quiet, comfortable, uninterrupted space in which to do it.
- **Think** on the questions we raised earlier in the chapter.
- **Imagine** it's seven years into the future, and write down everything you are doing in as much detail as you can.
- **Dream** big and do not censor or edit yourself in any way. Just keep going and writing down anything that comes into your stream of consciousness until nothing else comes out.
- **Create** something visual to represent the life you've imagined.

Then, set aside five minutes a day, either first thing in the morning or before you go to bed, to look at what you created and visualize yourself living this life using the handy Dos and Don'ts above.

REBUILDING YOUR MINDSET

What do you water right now in your life? Because whatever you water will take over your garden. Whatever you water will grow; whatever you irrigate with your imagination will grow.
— Patience Johnson

Mindset is not woo-woo, positive-thinking fluff. In fact, there's nothing more concrete, practical, and powerful than learning how to put your mind to work in service of living the life your heart desires.

Developing your mindset is like planting seeds. Plant them, and then coax them to grow by watering them, in this case with your thoughts. Once you get into the habit of coaching yourself to keep at it, learn what you can from each situation and move forward, generally staying focused on your own effort and attitude. Optimism, inner confidence, and peace will become your default settings. And the things you put your effort into will bloom just like the plants and flowers you tend in your garden.

This chapter is about three types of mindset shifts and how we can practice them to support our recovery from burnout. They are growth mindset, should versus choose, and cultivating a sabbatical-style mindset and way of being. But first, let's take a lesson from nature.

RAFTING – MINDSET LESSONS FROM THE RIVER

Several years ago, our family went on a four-day rafting and camping adventure on Oregon's Rogue River. Our kids were eleven and thirteen, and it was a blast to be off-grid for a few days, immersed into the experience. The lead guide was excellent—calm, firm, and trustworthy. She taught us a safety concept in rafting that has a wonderful metaphorical significance to life.

"Look positive" in rafting means: Focus on where you want to go, not on the danger zones. If you're rafting, you want to focus your eyes, attention, and even body posture toward the line you wish to cut through the river, which will offer safe passage. You don't want to look at obstructions like rocks, branches, or areas where the currents are pushing down underwater, since where you look is the direction you'll go.

> Where we choose to focus our attention is such an essential part of mindset training. When we apply our rafting lesson to life, we see that "look positive" means focusing on what you want to accomplish, where you want to go in life.

It could mean keeping to a daily fitness routine as part of a strength goal and focusing on the daily effort and results involved instead of the anticipated pain of failing or the lack of fitness that would result from sitting all day.

Focusing on all the reasons that our heart's desires are impossible, unreasonable, unearned, challenging, or scary will cause us to unwittingly amplify those things, and increase the likelihood they will become true. We're not guaranteed to achieve a goal simply by wanting it and working toward it, but at least we've invited it into our realm of possibility.

Not believing it's possible and not taking baby steps each day toward it, however, does guarantee we won't get it. Henry Ford once said, "Whether you think you can or think you can't, you're right," underscoring the simple foundational requirement for doing anything, anytime, anywhere: the belief that we can.

GROWTH MINDSET

Mindset is everything, so they say, and it's a pretty strong foundation for sure. Growth mindset means, at its most basic level, that we know we can always learn and grow, and thus we are never fully stuck and have never truly failed.

> A huge part of growth mindset involves focusing on your efforts and personal growth (the things you can control) instead of obsessing over outcomes, which are a combo of your effort and the actions and impacts of the rest of the world (which you can't control).

It also requires internal comfort with yourself and your agency, letting go of the external pressures, and seating your locus of personal power within.

The book *Mindset* by Dr. Carol Dweck is so encouraging, affirming, and inspiring that after I read it, I became convinced I needed to work to promote its teachings. There's an organization called Mindset Works that does just that, and I reached out to them and pitched them to join their team. They responded and we met a few times to discuss some possibilities before I ultimately decided to launch a consulting business in my previous field of housing development.

Since then, the book has had a profound influence on my life and approach to everything—from work to cultivating new skills and interests to parenting and even to relationships. The practice of building and applying growth mindset is a lifelong one and a muscle very much worth developing. Everything you really want to do goes from being "not possible" or "I could never" to "I learn and grow all the time" and "I haven't done it *yet*, but I know I can figure this out."

Relieving myself of the pressure to know everything from the outset, to be good at things before even working at them, and to appear capable and talented to others was essential.

Without releasing all that baggage, I'd never have been able to open my mind to the constant learning, iteration, and missteps required to conceive of and grow my business, to better nurture my relationships with family and friends, and to muster the courage and perseverance to finally learn guitar.

I took weekly lessons for the first year to get some guitar basics down. I'd never played an instrument before, and here I was in my 40s getting schooled by my preteen classmates. Yikes.

I wrote a song based on a family travel snafu at a museum in France called "No Merci" and shared it with my teacher, Randy. He looked a little confused, informed me that some of my chord combos were discordant, and suggested changes. I informed him that that was my intention! It was the artistic brilliance of the song!

Only someone not afraid to suck, for a while at least, could have the nerve to keep at it long enough to improve. (I now know more about how chords relate to each other and understand that my song was somewhat of a musical assault on my teacher's ears, but hey, you gotta start somewhere.)

Mindset training gives you the mental tools to allow yourself to keep learning and growing without the crushing weight of judgment.

Growth mindset sounds like:

- Self-determination, self-possession, driven by internal values and what lights you up.
- Having faith in oneself to creatively solve problems; persistence and agility in the face of challenges.
- Realizing that the "unknown is where possibility glitters" (Michelle Obama) and regarding it with openness, curiosity, and excitement instead of terror.
- Spending energy on things you can control (effort, attitude, building healthy habits).
- The ability to focus on a vision for success (eyes on the prize).
- Embracing missteps, experimentation, iteration, and evolution as essential ingredients for doing anything interesting or new.

Fixed mindset sounds like:

- Self-neglect, blaming others, making excuses.
- Being driven by external expectations and obsession with the approval of others.
- Perfectionism.
- Impatience and a tendency to give up when new skills are not easily mastered; low resilience.
- Avoidance of exploration and healthy risks, sticking with the "known devil" at all times even if doesn't work well or is dull.
- Stressing about outcomes and other people (factors outside of your control).
- Getting stuck on specific and conventional solutions or pathways; rigid thinking.

One more thing about mindset: None of us approaches *everything* from either a growth or fixed mindset. We may approach certain things with openness and curiosity and other things with rigidity and negative self-talk. The best part about growth mindset is that growth mindset *itself* can be practiced and strengthened in all realms of life. So, if you catch yourself saying "I could never do that" about something you're deep-down longing to do, pause and reframe the statement to "I can't do that, *yet*, but I'm sure excited to try."

SHOULD VERSUS CHOOSE – A POWERFUL DISTINCTION

What's your relationship with the word "should"?

For years, mine was fraught. To be honest, it still is sometimes. My single mom taught me and my sister to be strong but also to be "good" and service-oriented children. These qualities are great—to a certain point. After that, they become obstacles to knowing and caring for ourselves, as we become so habituated to putting the expectations of others and society first that we lose touch with our own inner compass.

Sure, there are some basic things we *should* do to build a healthy foundation: make enough money to pay the bills, make time and space to care for ourselves and our loved ones, stay off the hard drugs... But what about the countless other "shoulds" we've absorbed over the years from culture, school, work, family, friends? The things that often dictate our choices and actions, even if they are not actually related to our well-being or that of our loved ones or even our communities?

Here are a few you might be familiar with, particularly if you are a woman:

- You should be less emotional.
- You should care more and take care of everyone's needs.
- You should be grateful you even have a job at all.

- You should lean in to get that promotion—you're not putting yourself out there enough.
- You shouldn't be so braggy and overconfident.
- You should be assertive but not bitchy.
- You should be youthful but not inexperienced.
- You should have executive presence and gravitas but not be old.
- You should dress your age.
- You should really maintain your looks better (yes to plastic surgery, no to gray hair).
- You should control your feelings and never get angry or hysterical.
- You should stand up for yourself better and fight back; if not, you allowed the abuse.

What about those? And so many like them? The ones that keep you "in your place," that keep you small and quiet, that urge you to ignore your instincts and put yourself last on your to-do list, that keep you from making waves, and that often lead you to betray yourself in the interest of complying, serving, or achieving that elusive (and ultimately imprisoning) state of dependence on external approval. Never mind that approval and perfection are impossible to achieve, since most of the expectations of women contradict each other and there's no way to do it all "right." Just google America Ferrera's speech in the blockbuster *Barbie* movie; she captures this toxic dynamic beautifully.

Let's visit one more category of "shoulds"—the ones related to external status. You know them. The ones that say you should have a certain job title *by now* or live in a certain-sized house in a certain zip code or drive a certain car or have a certain brand of handbag or watch or take vacations that cost a ton in certain places so you can prove your worth on Instagram. The list of stuff our commercialized culture would *love* for you to relentlessly prioritize and seek to acquire is long, and the pressure from peers can be intense.

This isn't a diatribe against having "nice things" or earning a fabulous living, BTW. I love my fancy, insanely good smelling face cream, our comfy mid-century modern home, adventures traveling to interesting places, and I'm a full believer in investing in quality, long-lasting furniture, clothing, electronics, etc. I also think we should be paid appropriately and well for our contributions in the work world and raise whatever hell we need to make that a reality.

It's just that we often get caught up in what *others* think we should have but that maybe we personally couldn't care less about. And this can keep us tethered hard to the golden handcuff hamster wheel of sacrificing everything we hold dear to put paid work first and make as much money as possible, only to spend it all on stuff that doesn't contribute to our health, well-being, happiness, or help us nurture the relationships that matter most.

Releasing our need to prove to the outside world through status symbols that we're worthy allows us far greater mental, emotional, and financial freedom to consciously choose how to spend our time, energy, and money on people and things that bring us joy now and to build the future our heart desires.

These desires will naturally shift during the various ages, stages, and earning levels of our lives.

For example, when we are working less but are richer in time, we might choose to vacation closer to home and spend the time learning to make things instead of paying for shortcuts and time savers, venturing further again when finances allow.

The most important thing is that we remember our worth is never up for debate; it doesn't require anyone else to confirm it. It's been there all along, waiting for us to notice and nurture it, and to make choices and act from that deep connection to our intuition, value, and values.

Friends, I invite you to take this opportunity to declare your independence from the word *should*. This simple reframe restores our agency and puts us back in the power seat of our own lives.

For each of these questions below, if you really don't know the answer, you may be a bit disconnected from your intuition (your core sense of inner knowing). Don't worry; part of this practice is getting reacquainted with it. If you feel uncertain, close your eyes, and breathe deeply. Observe how your body reacts to each alternative under consideration. Does one invoke feelings of aversion or revulsion? Does one spark interest or a sense of lightness? Imagine yourself living into each option a few months or years into the future; how does that feel?

The first step in dealing with the "shoulds" of our lives is simply to notice when they appear in our thoughts and words.

Each time your mind offers up statements about things you allegedly *should* do, pause and ask yourself some questions to see how you really feel about them and what you actually prefer to do.

- Is this true?
- Who says?
- Is it essential?
- Is it healthy and safe for you?

Once you've asked those questions to weed out the stuff that merits a hard and fast rejection, ask these questions of the shoulds that remain to help you decide how to proceed:

- Do I want to do this?
- What might I prefer instead?
- What feels right?
- What feels true to myself?
- What might happen if I choose differently?

- What choice leads me closer to a life spent on what matters most to me?

So, if you were in charge of your own choices (which you are!), which option would you most want to pursue? What matters most to you right now? What will you look back on in one, three, or five years and be happy that you spent time, energy, and money on today? What do you *choose* to do?

Now here comes the hard part: Release your attachment to the unhealthy "shoulds." They are merciless, and if you allow them, they will bludgeon you into submission.

Old thought patterns and mindsets die hard and require gentle (repeated) practice to rewire your brain. Accept that regardless of your choices, it's impossible to satisfy everyone or to know how each choice will exactly play out into the future. Make the best choice you can with the information you have now. Value yourself, your worth, your health, and your inner compass. These will guide you toward building a life in alignment with who and what matters most, one choice and moment at a time. If you determine that the choice you made isn't working as hoped in a week, month, or year, reevaluate and if needed, make a new one! Flex your choices as needed to address changes in circumstances and information.

This simple mindset shift has worked wonders for me and my clients in fueling empowerment because it positively impacts how we think about the way we engage with the world.

SHOULD:

- is external pressure-focused
- evokes guilt and shame
- feels heavy and forced

- takes energy away

CHOOSE:

- is internal-values driven
- invites us to contemplate our life choices with agency
- asks "What do I actually want?" and "What will I prioritize?"
- restores energy and authentic power
- feels energizing

Should we go for that walk in the fresh air, or do we *choose* to do so (or not to)?

Should we apply for that exciting (and challenging) new role, or do we *choose* to do so (or not to)?

Should we show up at that after-work networking event, or do we *choose* to do so (or not to)?

The ultimate question to ask ourselves as we make these decisions has three parts: What do we truly want? What supports our well-being? How we want to live our lives? Once we know these three things, we can choose accordingly and take ownership for the choice, leaving the chastising voices in our head out of the discussion.

In her gem of a collection of short stories *Wouldn't Take Nothing for My Journey Now,* Maya Angelou wrote: "The woman who survives intact and happy must be at once tender and tough. She must have convinced herself that she, her values, and her choices are important. In a time and world where males hold sway and control, the pressure upon women to yield their rights-of-way is tremendous. And it is under those very circumstances that the woman's toughness must be in evidence."

Talk about self-possession. Maya Angelou had it in spades. If I could meet one person who is no longer on this earth, it would be her.

CULTIVATING A SABBATICAL-STYLE MINDSET AND WAY OF BEING

Cultivating a sabbatical-style mindset and way of being starts with learning about the power of growth mindset, how to develop it, and how to apply it to your life so that it paints every choice, attitude, and action you take with a shimmer of possibility. It continues with strengthening the sense of agency we bring to our everyday thoughts and decisions, which helps us choose what is right for us rather than being pummeled by the pressure of "should." It's about understanding at your core that you have everything you need to create your most meaningful life inside of you, right now at this very moment, no matter where you are. And that once you've learned how to use it, it's up to you to nourish and sustain it.

Those who hear about my story of sabbatical leave ask me if a literal sabbatical is needed to recover from burnout. My answer? It depends on the severity of your burnout and what you do during your time away.

It's possible to trot all over the world looking for life's answers outside yourself, come back with some cool adventures under your belt and go back to the grind and your same old self-neglecting practices, habits, mindsets. It's also possible to learn and apply the practices, habits, and mindsets of self-care and beyond to self-possession here and now, wherever you are.

Depending on how far down the burnout rabbit hole you are, you may find varying forms of "time-out" to be restorative to you. Early-stage burnout folks can take shorter breaks and incorporate restorative practices into their everyday lives more readily. Mid-stage burnout folks might need a longer reprieve for their adjustments to gain traction. Those deeper into burnout, like I was, may need a stronger intervention, and that can take many forms both close to home and far away.

Regardless of where you land on the burnout spectrum, the practices in this book can be applied and offer you all the tools you need to reset, restore, rejuvenate, and reconnect with yourself and others. They apply to all the various forms and timeframes of sabbatical-style rest and burnout recovery. They can expand in scope and time as your schedule allows—from a brief, weekly exercise to be done while still working to a longer-term practice while on a literal sabbatical leave.

No matter which you engage in, one of the lasting outcomes we're aiming to achieve is a sabbatical-style mindset and way of being, which you can take with you anywhere.

If practiced and nourished, it can last for a lifetime. It will protect you from future trips down the lava-ridden volcano of burnout and keep you locked into a state of centered self-possession.

REDEFINING AND CLAIMING A SABBATICAL-STYLE WAY OF BEING

The old definition of a sabbatical is a period of paid leave granted to a university teacher for study or travel, traditionally one year for every seven years worked. People seek out a sabbatical leave to enjoy deep rest, rekindle their creativity, fuel inspiration, deepen connection with their core selves and their loved ones, and seek what may be out there beyond their limited field of vision, to name a few reasons.

Here's a new definition for sabbatical that I created as a way to broaden access to this extremely restorative concept: A sabbatical is a gift you give yourself to rest, recover, restore, rejuvenate, reconnect, and rejoice. These are the ingredients of a new mindset and way of being that can be cultivated and enjoyed now. And although more and more companies are offering paid sabbatical leaves of varying lengths to their longer-term staff (this is amazing!), it's actually a practice anyone can learn and apply to their everyday lives whether working or not, at home or abroad.

And if you do make that leap to disconnect for a bit from your established routine, practicing this mindset will ensure that you get the most out of your time away, and return truly restored and resourced to transform your fresh learnings into sustained and lasting well-being.

You might know the word sabbatical is related to Sabbath, which refers to the biblical day of rest. In the book, *Sabbath* by Wayne Muller, he writes: "Sabbath does not require us to leave home, change jobs, or leave the world of ordinary life. It is not spiritually superior to our work. The practice is to find the point at which, having rested, we do our work with greater ease and joy, and bring healing and delight to our endeavors."

Dr. Saundra Dalton-Smith has an excellent Ted Talk and book on the seven types of rest we all need (physical, mental, spiritual, emotional, sensory, social, and creative). We can learn to incorporate these at any time, not consigning them to a few weeks a year when we escape the grind for a vacation, retreat, or holiday break. These practices get easier and more natural over time, nurturing us and allowing us to show up more fully, present, and alive in our work and personal lives.

Having taken time and space away to heal from the American culture rat race of everyday working and living, the notion that we can and would greatly benefit from incorporating restoration into our everyday lives checks out. It's about putting this new mindset to work to create a life from which we don't need to escape, one conscious decision at a time.

You know what else I learned? I had what I needed within me all along to reclaim my sense of self, my connection with others, and my physical and mental well-being. I just needed to learn how to use it.

We don't need to eject from our lives and have our own *Eat, Pray, Love* year of escapism. (Although that does sound amazing, and no shade if you make that a reality for yourself.) There *is* something to be said for literally removing ourselves from our day-to-day grind. It can be easier to toss out the old routines and habits that are not serving you and try out new ones when you are in a new place with new people and new experiences.

However, as I learned, even if long-term travel becomes part of your journey, as it was for me and my family for a time, the mindsets and attitudes you carry follow you across the border. There's no escaping the deep dive within to reflect and get really clear on what matters most. You must ditch the things, thoughts, and actions that are holding you back and then rebuild your mindset and habits toward creating the life you want.

ADVICE FOR READERS PREPARING FOR A LITERAL SABBATICAL

The sabbatical I took was not one where I was paid and planned to return. In my case, I quit my job of fifteen years in order to recover. And it took me and my husband nearly two years year to save, cut expenses, and plan for how to live on quite a bit less income for a while. You'd be amazed what can be cut if you really want and need to make that happen, and how a simpler, less costly lifestyle can actually feel quite restorative when you suddenly have the gift of time, which you've dreamed of for a long time. So many of our costs went to buying things and services that saved time, and when I suddenly had lots more of it, we let the time-savers go and just focused on time together. This gave me a chance to get my mental and physical house in order.

Here's an unpleasant reality I'd like to prepare you for. Aside from announcing my leave from work, the only other time in my life I've received so much annoying unsolicited advice was while pregnant. Let me tell you: people feel quite comfortable asking personal questions, getting in your personal space, and offering weird "damned if you do, damned if you don't" commentary to pregnant people, such as:

- "You're going to eat *that?*"
- "Carrying twins?" (No)
- "You know you shouldn't wear heels."
- "Are you sure you're okay? You're pretty compact for a pregnant person."
- "Oh that name you picked out is… interesting."
- "Why are you still working? You know children need their moms at home."
- "You're taking leave already? I worked up to the day of my delivery!"
- "You're only getting six weeks of maternity leave? My neighbor got twelve."
- "Have you heard [insert urban legend or conspiracy theory here] is bad for babies?"
- "You're not going to stay in that tiny house, are you?"

For whatever reason, everyone has an opinion when they see a woman pregnant. The judgements are endless, and rest assured, they show up with even greater vigor when you opt to press pause in life and in your career to reclaim yourself.

There's apparently something unacceptable and unseemly in our culture about women "selfishly" seeing to their own needs and desires. In fact, if I ever revealed the stuff I did purely for my own time-wasting frivolous enjoyment (instead of in service of others), looks of disapproval came from everywhere.

Don't let them derail you. Breathe, pause, focus on what *you* want and need. If you're out of practice doing this, it will feel like a near-impossible feat of Herculean proportions. Hold steady. You got this far in life by figuring shit out, and you'll do it again this time, solving challenges as they come, one at a time. You do *not* have to have every move for the next five years figured out like some chess savant. That's not even possible, so ditch the idea now and save yourself lots of self-induced agony.

My kids learned very young in school to take mean or unproductive comments and literally throw them into their mental trash can. This is accomplished by putting your hand on your hip to make an open triangle between your arm and body. Then you take the verbal trash in your other hand and toss it through the opening. Viola! Bye bye, nasty feedback.

Here's some of the loud, uninvited, bad advice, and side-eye commentary you may expect from others as to the demise of your life and career if you decide, in ways big or small, to go off-script and see to your needs *before* trying to drain the ocean of serving everyone else or checking off all the status boxes of success.

Stuff to put into your mental trash can:

- "You can't have even a small gap on your resume. You'll be unhirable, and your career will be forever off track."
- "Never leave a job without knowing every detail about your next move."
- "What if you never find another job, or at least another good one?"
- "Everyone will think of you as a mommy-track unserious professional."
- "You can't take your kids out of school to travel. You'll ruin their friendships and path to college."
- "Don't you want a bigger and better house (and engagement ring) now that you're older?"

- "Must be nice to be able to have [some random thing you gave yourself or time off the grind]. All *my* money goes to my kids' education."
- "You're learning guitar? Wow you have a lot of free time."
- "I think it's time you considered Botox." (Okay, this one is not exactly work-leave related, but a coworker did suggest this to me on my last week at work. She was apparently concerned my career would be over due to the lines on my forehead from my never-ending facial expressions that reveal my thoughts before I ever even open my mouth. Ah, the joys of midlife womanhood.)
- "You're not coming to [xyz unnecessary event, volunteer thing, or random 'obligation']? Why? What could possibly be more important? We're relying on you!"
- "You are not quitting that job! I rely on you for support!"

Another strategy I use to help respond to things (or ignore them) from a much more level and dispassionate place is one I learned in dealing with family situations like awkward holiday get-togethers. If the family drama gets too hot and triggers irritation, defensiveness, and reactivity, I pretend I'm hanging out with someone else's family, just a fly on the wall. You know how when you're at your friend's house and their family is acting up, and not only does it not bother you much, it's actually kind of amusing and validating?

It's amazing how much a little distance can help us lighten up and see that no matter what, we are grown women, and we can decide what we want and need to do, regardless of what the endlessly opinionated peanut gallery thinks about it.

Expect feedback from all angles, all places, and all people. While some family members and friends will see the crumbling parts of you that you are trying to piece together and offer grace and support, others will throw blame, shame, and shade. You'll shake out real quick who to invite into your inner circle during this next phase of your life.

I'll admit that sometimes the statements people make have nuggets of truth. Consider the source, intent, and value of each statement to decide whether to give it some weight or toss it into your mental trash can.

Remember, the things people say and do mostly reflect what is going on inside of them. These folks do not have any special, crystal ball insight, nor do they know more about your life than you do. They are projecting their own fears, biases, beliefs, judgements, personal preferences and interests, and even jealousy onto you. You do not have to accept any of this input if it doesn't offer some productive use or insight for you.

THE BOTTOM LINE

A sabbatical-style mindset is one in which you know in your bones that you have everything you need to create your most meaningful life inside of you, right now at this very moment, no matter where you are. It's deciding to give *yourself* the gifts of rest, recovery, restoration, rejuvenation, reconnection, and rejoicing. And understanding that once you've learned how to use it, it's up to you to nourish and sustain it for a lifetime.

REFLECTION ACTIVITIES

What's something you've always wanted to try but:

- You didn't think you could since you have no "innate talent."
- You thought it was too late or you're too old.
- You were told you were bad at it, so you never tried.

- You figured you'd never be able to learn due to some special level of incompetence, impatience, or embarrassment. (Why are we so mean to ourselves?)

What's something you have tried that you're kind of *meh* at but are now willing to put in the effort to improve?

What's one thing you've been grudgingly doing because you think you *should*, but it's not actually necessary and is weighing on you like a set of brass, 1980s shoulder pads?

What does sabbatical mean to you? What could it look like for you? Remember, sabbaticals can be small parts of your day instead of full-fledged escapes. How can you cultivate a sabbatical-style mindset and way of being into your everyday life by giving yourself the gifts of rest, recovery, restoration, rejuvenation, reconnection, and rejoicing?

REBUILDING YOUR SCHEDULE

Do what you can, where you are, with what you have.
— Arthur Ashe

You've probably read or heard it said that time is our most precious asset—the only one that's truly irreplaceable—and yet it's one we give, spend (and often waste) far more freely than we do physical assets like money or possessions. Our time is everything, and how we choose to spend it says a lot about our values and priorities. Now that we've gotten rid of some freeloading stuff on our calendars, let's talk about rebuilding our schedule with intention and with our own well-being front and center on our list of things that matter.

INGREDIENTS FOR WELL-BEING

Ripping down the wooded, single-track trail, leaves and gravel crunching satisfyingly underfoot with each leap, I realized I couldn't remember the last time I'd felt so free and had so much unbridled fun. I imagine I looked a bit like Phoebe from that episode of *Friends* where she runs wildly through Central Park—arms flailing, joy palpable.

This is how I felt at my first trail running race through the redwoods in Oakland, California. Like Phoebe, I ran down the rooted, rutted dirt trail with a mixture of wild abandon and balance, focused intently on the location of each footfall while at the same time immersed in the experience of moving fast through the forest. Looking like a maniac didn't bother me a bit. It was exhilarating to find such a source of joy that would end up becoming an essential component to my health in body, mind, and spirit.

It wasn't until my 40s that I'd realize my love for trail running and get serious about regularly and heartily tending to my own needs, inside and out—serious about taking good, strong care of myself as a pathway to self-worth, self-possession, and living with joy and purpose.

> I learned that the more I took care of myself, the more goodness I had to share with others, and that the opposite is also true.

Fast forward to March 2020, when the pandemic lockdowns began. The kids and I were working and schooling from home, and my husband went to work in person with hefty safety protocols in place. We were afraid to visit our loved ones nearby, to go to the grocery store, or even to eat an apple that hadn't been thoroughly bleached. And even though we took up acrylic painting, bread making, evening walks, Kahoot parties with family and friends online, and all the other sweet and connecting activities homebound families did during that time, by May my nervous system was getting fried with the constant masking, cleaning, vigilance, isolation, and mental preparation for imminent death.

There's a natural hillside area near our house we'd hiked in as a family a few times, but I wasn't sure of how the trails connected or if it was safe to run alone. We have coyotes in our area, but I was more concerned about threats of the human variety that lone women trail runners have learned to deal with, and for the record, *should not* have to. Now there's an appropriate use of the word should.

Side note: When I traveled to Ireland for a weeklong trail running adventure, all of the American women had experienced some form of harassment, threats of violence, or worse while out on the trail. The Irish women were horrified, as this was not their experience at all. One woman from the American South even ran with a pistol tucked into her shorts to protect herself after repeated threats from a well-heeled and well-connected man in her town who wouldn't back off. (Reporting him would have resulted in retribution for her, not him.) This is a different story for another day, and I'm sure you know all too well the lengths women with the nerve to run outside the lines go to for their mere survival. This constant vigilance is an invisible contributor to the mental and emotional exhaustion elements of burnout.

Even with these concerns, I knew I needed to create a healthy daily routine, preferably in nature, to help my body and mind navigate the constant stress of living and raising a tween and teen through a pandemic. Each morning before work, I ventured out and each day explored a little further. Eventually I learned the trails and got familiar with the other folks on them and pieced together a few routes. After a month or two it was a solid habit—one I looked forward to each day.

Keeping my word to myself to continue it (and protect it as a high priority) was an outward expression of self-worth, self-care, self-love, and—if I'm being honest, basic self-preservation and survival. It's still an essential element of my helpful daily routine, though now I sub in swimming or Krav Maga a day or two a week instead.

This chapter is all about the importance of finding your ingredients for well-being and cementing in your own helpful daily routine—

your set of habits that keep you centered, healthy, and resilient. I cannot overstate how essential it is to thoughtfully use your time in service of creating the life you so dearly want to live, and the importance of setting yourself up for success in the morning.

The continuum of well-being works like this: Your thoughts build your mindset, which fuels your actions, which culminate into habits, which, if done with care and intention, over time create a life worth living.

Habits are the ingredients of our recipe for well-being.

GARBAGE IN, GARBAGE OUT

In the real estate development world, we would often use the phrase "garbage in, garbage out" to refer to the reliability of construction pricing as a direct result of the quality and level of completeness of the architectural plans.

This concept is also true in our lives.

We eat junk food, sit all day, doom scroll on social media, consume soul-crushing media, spend time with people who treat us like crap, etc. And then we wonder why we feel like shit—stressed out, overwhelmed, no energy, low confidence, low motivation.

Happily, the opposite is also true. Quality ingredients make a delicious meal. By adjusting each of these choices (one at a time), we concoct our own recipe for well-being. Once we discover the ingredients that work best for us, we can make them into habits, and the inevitable outcome will be:

- Increased well-being
- Better physical and mental health
- Healthier relationships

- Confidence, motivation, and inspiration
- A return of our zest for life

HABITS ARE THE INGREDIENTS OF OUR RECIPE FOR WELL-BEING

Continuing with our food metaphor: You know how, on every cooking show and movie, there's a vignette with the head chef at a market personally picking out their ruby-red tomatoes, crisp greens, fresh-caught fish, and such? Just as the success of their finished dishes is a result of the quality of each element that went into it, so too with our lives. It seems so basic, so dull, and even so maddening to think that in many ways, setting ourselves up for success is as simple as establishing quality life habits—but it's true.

It's time to get into the nitty gritty of crafting a lifestyle that supports our well-being, inside and out. Habits are the building blocks of our solid foundation. Without helpful ones, we quickly melt into quicksand the minute that challenges, uncertainties, and life stressors arise (and they always do).

Over time, our habits become our lives.

Did you know, the average person spends four-plus hours per day (10 years of their lives) performing mindless habits on autopilot? For many of us, the thoughts and activities that arise during those hours are not intentionally chosen and nurtured. As a result, we don't spend our time and energy building a life that matters to us and fulfills us at a core level. We simply cave to the loudest expectation from others or do what seems most convenient or easy—like scrolling through our phone, endlessly binging news or other entertainment, or engaging in other unhelpful coping mechanisms we picked up along the way to soothe or numb the discomfort and uncertainty.

Our brain is trying to conserve energy by not thinking through every single decision, and when we're burned out, we don't have the energy it takes to notice unhelpful habits and get rid of them, much less to then replace them with habits that serve us.

This is perhaps the most common challenge I come across with clients, friends, and certainly in my own life. How can we do the things we know we need to do to take proper care of ourselves when we're already bone- and soul-tired? It feels like there's no room in our minds or schedules to even consider the question.

You know when you're at a point where doing anything at all outside the core essentials for survival feels like a monumental task? When adding a few fun tips you read on the internet or a magazine, like walking in nature, switching to tea, or doing adult coloring books, all feel like slapping a Band-Aid on a stab wound or adding a little oil to your car when the engine has exploded? (I tried this in college when I ran my poor little orange 1969 VW bug with only AM radio into the ground). Do any of those actually help the stab wound or the exploded engine? No ma'am, they don't.

First, unless we dump some old habits, this just adds more stuff to feel bad about not doing to help ourselves. This is why self-care and the industry that has sprung up to sell our health to us often seem like an annoyance or even a scam. Who has time to add more stuff to the list?

Second, we're going to need a more systematic intervention to repair ourselves. Not even a particularly hard system, just a focused and consistent one—at least until our new self-maintenance program has become so ingrained that it has replaced the old, unchosen, self-defeating set of habits with a new set we now perform on autopilot and no longer need to work so hard to make happen. If we lock these habits in completely, they can become so natural and enjoyable they are simply part of our identity, requiring no thought or effort at all.

One of the ways burnout manifests in our lives and behavior is that our brains are too busy to make decisions at each moment of the day to support our own well-being. We get stuck in unhelpful coping patterns. We need fewer decisions to make, and a helpful structure is just the ticket. Here are some battle-tested, well-worn strategies for getting yourself on track.

HOW WE FORM AND CHANGE HABITS

According to the book, *The Power of Habit* by Charles Duhigg, there is a Golden Rule of habit formation. By understanding this, we can train our brains to ditch the not-so-helpful habits and embrace the helpful ones. We can support ourselves in the work of habit change with our mindset (belief we can do it), support (sharing our goals with account-ability partners), and autonomy (choosing to do it ourselves instead of succumbing to pressure or doing it because we think we should).

Anyone who recalls being a teenager knows full well how important autonomy is. Think for a moment about how you instantly recoil, as if you just stepped in vomit, the minute some do-gooder (like your parents, for instance), tells you how you should stop certain *bad* habits and add certain *good* ones. The truth is, we will make changes when *we* are good and ready and not a minute before.

Here's a quick summary of Duhigg's Golden Rule elements:

- Cue: the thing that triggers a certain behavior.
- Routine: the thing we do after the cue; also, the part we can swap for our preferred option.
- Reward: the thing we get from doing the behavior and the reason our brain wants to do it anyway.

Here's an example of how a person might use Duhigg's Golden Rule to swap a habit they are trying to let go of with a new one. I read about a man who was trying to quit smoking. Every time he felt a little anxious or unsettled, he went out to his yard and had a cigarette.

He had a little smoking zone out there since he wanted to keep the smoke away from his household. He put a weight bench out in that area and every time he got the urge to smoke, he went out to the same spot and lifted weights for five minutes, the same amount of time it took to smoke.

In the old routine: the Cue was anxiety, the Routine was to smoke, and the Reward was relaxation.

In the new routine: the Cue was the same (anxiety), the Routine was to lift weights, and the Reward was the same (relaxation).

He simply swapped out the Routine (replacing smoking with lifting weights). Not only did he quit smoking, but he also added some exercise into his daily routine, gaining mental and physical health benefits in the process. Amazing!

James Clear's book *Atomic Habits* is another staple text on this topic. He says if you get one percent better each day for one year, you'll end up thirty-seven times better at the end. He's a master at making the case for the power of tiny steps of incremental movement toward whatever it is we want to invite into our lives, and his nifty calculation proves this.

We all intuitively know from memorizing our times tables in third grade or from our piano- or basketball-playing days that the boring old concept of practice is how we gradually gain skill, comfort, and ease with new things. It's how we convert awkward beginnings into smooth-performing badassery.

Consistency is key, and even a few minutes a day adds up like crazy over time.

Ten minutes a day is better than sixty minutes once a week—at least, that's what my kids' piano teacher said, and every other expert on habits and skill-building will tell you the same thing.

A COMMON MORNING ROUTINE / HABIT STACK

Your morning routine, which can also be described as a morning habit stack, is simply a set of actions you perform upon waking, usually in the same order, before you head off to do the other various things on your agenda for the day.

Most of us stumble without much thought into our morning routine. Here's an example of a common habit stack which is not such a helpful start to the day. Many of these items, ahem, have been on my list many times over the years, so no judgment.

Wake up.

Lie in bed for a few minutes dreading work or worrying about kids, parents, health, finances, the broken dishwasher, environmental degradation, corruption in politics, the recession, threat of war, etc.

Reach for your phone and check email, social media, the news, your horoscope, the weather, etc.

Drag yourself to the kitchen to make coffee or tea.

Shower and get ready for work.

If you have kids, squeeze in getting them up, feeding them breakfast, making their lunches, and getting them off to school or daycare.

This routine takes at least an hour or two and sends you into your day drained of energy, already exhausted, cynical, stressed out, angry, and focused on how the world is going to hell in a handbasket. It seems easy enough, and maybe harmless, but not only does it involve spending time and energy on things that fail to nourish you, it robs you of precious energy you need to handle the demands, opportunities, and chances to connect meaningfully with others that the day may bring.

A NEW MORNING ROUTINE / HABIT STACK 30 DAY CHALLENGE

Here's a morning routine/habit stack challenge that has worked wonders for me and my clients. Doing this will build a solid foundation of mental and physical health and set you up for success in everything else you do.

Think back to activities and habits you've tried in the past that have helped center and support you. Make a list of the most useful ones (I'll suggest some below if you'd like some ideas).

Do these activities every day in a habit stack for the next thirty days to give them a chance to become actual habits you no longer need to plan or think about. It takes at least that long to move past your brain's resistance to change and its clever ability to talk you into keeping with the status quo. A stable daily routine also saves you the mental and emotional energy of making decisions at every moment of every day as to what to do next and sends you into your day feeling energized, centered, healthy, and accomplished.

Here's a sample morning routine for you to consider.

Wake up.

Breathe. Take a few deep breaths to enter the day in peace.

Appreciate. Take a few moments to think about how you want to show up in the world today, something or someone you feel appreciation for, and something that is going well and "right."

Drink. A full glass of water (plus tea or coffee if you like these).

Reflection. I recommend doing **one** of these two options, though some people are really early risers and do both).

Journal two to three pages (free-flowing stream of consciousness, no editing or judging). You'll be amazed what useful info bubbles up. Julia Cameron, author of *The Artist's Way*, calls these "morning pages."

Ten-minute guided meditation (using the Calm app, Insight timer, Kristin Neff's free self-compassion ones, the Body Scan described in chapter 3), or plain old sitting still and following your breath in and out; allow your thoughts to pass through without getting into debate with them.

Run or walk outside. Sometimes I sub in a swim or a YouTube exercise video to do inside the house; there are useful videos on everything from boxing to yoga to Pilates to dancing to core-strengthening. Just pick what you like and do some kind of movement each day. Exercise is the number one best thing you can do to support your well-being. Seriously. Even thirty minutes a day will result in significant improvements in your sleep, mental health, and physical health.

Get ready for work/the day. Shower, dress, and do what you need to be physically ready.

Optional. *After* all of the above are done, spend fifteen to twenty minutes on your favorite social media, horoscope, or other fun thing on your phone (only if you like to do this).

Final bonus tip. Read a favorite inspiring quote or mantra to start your day off in a powerful state of mind. I put mine at the top of my calendar on daily repeat, so I see it first thing upon opening my computer.

Arrange the elements that work best for you into your preferred order. Again, people with caretaking responsibilities will need to add those activities in the spots that work best for them.

If you've added the visualization activity to your life (as described in chapter 5), you can do it either in the morning and add it to your routine or do it before bed.

Notice I omit breakfast, since everyone is different in how and when they like to have their first meal of the day. Put that in where you want to. Some folks are super into intermittent fasting, and Dr. Mindy Pelz's books and YouTube videos are super helpful on this if you're considering it.

I like to make things easy for myself where possible, and breakfast is one way I do it. I get these pre-prepped frozen smoothie packs that have fruit, vegetables, seeds, and are packed with lots of great nutrients to start your day. I add yogurt or nut butter or sometimes just plain water, and after a minute in the blender I have a decent breakfast to start the day.

My family really hates the green smoothie variety, and say it looks and smells like grass. That is, until Snoop Dogg released his awesome cookbook, which includes a recipe for a green "Smoovie" with coconut water, greens, and fruit. My son bought the cookbook as he wanted to raise his cooking game and since he's into fitness and being the best athlete he can be, he's now reconsidering the merits of the green smoothie. But only because Snoop said it was cool.

Research on habit formation suggests that stacking habits like we've done here is an excellent way to train your brain to do them one after another in a helpful autopilot formation. You may already do some of these things and can continue as you were, just swapping in the reflection activity in place of the time on your phone, for example.

Setting the tone for your day rather than letting your phone do it for you gives you back your sense of agency, self-possession, and control over your own destiny.

Our phones can add so much convenience and entertainment to our lives, and those can be quite positive. But if left unchecked, they can easily gobble up time we'll ultimately wish we'd spent elsewhere.

Side note: "Check the News Feed of Doom" isn't on this list. I *highly* recommend you ditch this, period, and see how you feel. Our human brains have not evolved sufficiently to process or manage in healthy ways the trauma of billions of people or even an onslaught of sarcasm, negativity, and blame that passes as news media these days. Your feeling badly about something happening halfway around the world doesn't help solve that problem. It just helps you walk around under a dark cloud, spreading gloom wherever you go.

And the news rarely shows the simple acts of grace and humanity that also happen regularly around the world; this leaves us with a twisted and suspicious lens through which we live our lives. It robs us of essential energy we *need* if we're going to show up with love to support the people and causes dear to our hearts every day.

I cut out most general news consumption a few years ago and am far better off for it. I found a couple of trustworthy and professional sources to keep updated on the basics of being a reasonably informed human. The energy I used to spend scrolling and fretting has been reallocated to spreading love and care to those in my near and broader community, and I have chosen a few social justice, health-related, and youth development causes to support with my time, energy, and money.

If we all did that instead of wringing our hands for hours a day over the 1,000 pieces of bad news flooding our brains over which we have no control, the world would be a far better place.

In case you're feeling a little scolded, this mini diatribe is not to tech-shame you. If you've seen *The Social Dilemma*, you know our brains don't hold a candle to the mind-addicting firepower built into tech apps. We're not meant to win. They know how to hijack our attention, and since attention is what they're selling, they'll do anything to keep it. We've all read about the dopamine-addicting nature of the *like* button and how easy it is to get carried away with that little measurement of our status in the world. My husband and I watched the film with our teens so they could see our concerns were not just nutty overprotection but legitimate facts they can use to inform their decisions as they move into adulthood.

We can consciously choose to use the elements of technology that are helpful and healthy and serve our purpose, to delete the rest, and to set limits to keep from going down the hours-long scrolling rabbit hole. Just make sure you're actively choosing how to spend your precious (and limited) time and energy and not allowing technology to steal your day (and then feeling bad about it).

This new habit stack sets you on a solid foundation of thoughts and actions that support your well-being and move you into alignment with what matters most to you.

Then, having already accomplished so much in your morning, you can move on confidently and do whatever else you want and need to do for the day.

So, there you have it: the not-so-secret secret to building a healthy and resilient foundation for yourself is comprised of knitting together a handful of small, simple changes to your morning then sticking with them long enough for them to become habits.

At first, you can literally write them all out and put the list by your bed, but soon you'll have it all down and be able to blithely float through your morning on healthy autopilot. And while some of these take a bit of time, they are the kinds of actions that feed energy back to you many times over. You'll reap the benefits all day, especially if you ditch the not-so-helpful, soul-sucking habits as part of this process.

After a while, you'll settle in on your own unique ingredients in your recipe for well-being. Once you find what works, keep it, and fiercely protect the time and space for it so it can do its job and protect you. Trust me, once you've found your groove, you'll feel the difference. When you occasionally get off track, the solution will be to quietly and without fanfare just get back on and get going the next day.

BUT I HAVE NO TIME FOR ANY OF THIS! (A NOTE ON ASKING PERMISSION)

You may be saying to yourself, "This lady has literally no idea how much pressure there is on me to perform and how little freakin' time I truly have." You're right; we can only truly 100 percent understand our own life challenges (and frankly, sometimes I barely understand those)! But I *can* relate to having pushy people in my life and having way too much to do in way too little time, hoping others would suggest I take a load off and take more care of myself, having this never happen, and getting worn down to a sad little pulp as a result.

As Rear Admiral Grace Hopper (1906-1992) said: "It's easier to ask forgiveness than it is to get permission." She knew that in a huge bureaucracy, it can be extremely challenging to get affirmative support for even the most laudable of ideas. She received her PhD in mathematics from Yale, and was a pioneer in computer programming, software development, and the design and implementation of programming languages. She retired from the Navy at age seventy-nine, the oldest serving officer in the US armed forces. A legend in so many ways.

Interestingly, this principle applies to other realms of life too. And, assuming you're doing your best to make decent healthy choices for yourself, your household, and your job, you have nothing whatsoever to even ask forgiveness for (but I digress).

What I take her comment to mean as it applies to ditching the grind, recovering from burnout, and taking care of ourselves, is that it's up to us to make it happen. When we know permission is *never gonna come*, we have no choice but to take things into our own hands, take responsibility for our own choices and uses of time, and make the best decisions we can that allow us to stay true to ourselves and act from a place of self-possession—whether others ultimately like it or not.

Certain people and employers in your life are not likely to ever back off on their own or grant you permission to prioritize yourself (or your loved ones) in your own life. This is not because they are necessarily evil; it is because they're human, and most humans are focused on their own needs, gripes, and survival at a basic level. Also, this kind of permission is not actually theirs to give. It is for you to give yourself by valuing yourself and setting healthy boundaries.

Bottom line, the only person you are 100 percent responsible for is you. Do not wait for permission to do what you need to take care of your own needs and desires in life.

Move yourself up 100 or so rows on your to-do list, so you are at the top. This will take some skill-building in boundary-setting, like we covered in chapter 4. This way, when you run out of hours at the end of the day, the things left for another time are not the essential things you need to survive and thrive in this life.

I'm not claiming everyone's going to be super happy with not having you bend over backward for their every whim, but if you stay the course, they'll get used to it. Your job is to see to your own health and happiness; you can't control everyone else's.

REFLECTION ACTIVITIES

Ask yourself if what you're doing today is getting you closer to what you want to be doing tomorrow. What would your future self thank you for?

Map out your own morning routine habit stack and put it by your bed. Challenge yourself to stick with it for thirty days!

SUSTAINING PRACTICE: RESILIENCE

Grant me the serenity to accept the things I cannot change, courage to change the things I can, and wisdom to know the difference.
— Reinhold Niebuhr

A well-known Taoist story called "Maybe" captures the uncertainty inherent in human existence and helps us ease off the gas when it comes to labeling every single thing we encounter as good or bad. When we back off the labels, we also back off the accompanying urge to *do something about it*. We don't always have to work nights and weekends to change things. And sometimes the things we thought were "bad" are actually lessons, opportunities, insights, or shifts in a direction we ultimately appreciate.

This Taoist story tells of an old farmer who had worked his crops for many years. One day, his horse ran away. Upon hearing the news, his neighbors came to visit.

"Such bad luck," they said sympathetically.

"Maybe," the farmer replied.

The next morning the horse returned, bringing with it three other wild horses. "How wonderful!" the neighbors exclaimed.

"Maybe," replied the old man.

The following day, his son tried to ride one of the untamed horses, was thrown, and broke his leg. The neighbors again came to offer their sympathy for what they called his "misfortune."

"Maybe," answered the farmer.

The day after, military officials came to the village to draft young men into the army. Seeing that the son's leg was broken, they passed him by. The neighbors congratulated the farmer on how well things had turned out.

"Maybe," said the farmer.

I bet we've all had things happen to us that seemed bad; maybe they were really painful and terrible, but maybe they also pushed us to our growth edge. Maybe it led to a new experience or person we'd never have encountered if everything went as planned. Maybe that new thing ended up having a magic of its own.

A common example is a job layoff. It is unsettling, scary, and makes us question our worth, as well as how we're going to keep paying the bills.

Yet it is also an opportunity to try something new that you may have never tried if you were not pushed from the comfort of your nest.

A few years before my panic-ridden breakdown with my son's allergic reaction in the snowstorm, I knew something was not right. But instead of making shifts in my mindset, thoughts, actions, and habits toward self-possession, like I later learned to do, I spent a bunch of time and energy having myself checked out for everything under the sun, sure that if I could find the ailment responsible for all this, I could fix it. I was very externally focused, but I didn't realize I had some serious inner work to do.

One of the things I did was get fasting blood work, after which I fainted, going down like a tree and landing on the back of my head. I suffered a nasty concussion followed by months of vertigo (which still pops up here and there to this day). Apparently, according to my coworkers, it also resulted in a significantly reduced appetite for taking people's shit. It's like my filters got quite thin, and I had less and less of a problem telling folks to back off, setting boundaries, and caring less about all the ways people tried to force me into doing stuff I had little time for or interest in actually doing.

This incident required a few weeks of total rest, during which I mapped out in my mind some interim measures, starting with letting go of nonessential work events and volunteer commitments. The changes I made were ultimately so minor, though, that my burnout kept growing until the emergency incident forced a significant change.

Even after my sabbatical break began, it took a while to actually grasp the concept of taking time for myself and not immediately backfilling "free" time with more new stuff to do.

But eventually, I learned to slow the hell down and work on the garden, make a four-hour roast for our dinner, escape to the beach for a day, practice my guitar, play with my kids at the park until their little legs could play hide and seek no longer, and to do other life-affirming things.

CHANGE IS THE ONLY CONSTANT – AND OTHER ANNOYING TRUTHS

How do we accept that things are not required to go exactly as we want them to all the time at work, at home, and even in our own personal development? Insisting they do can get in the way of experiencing life in the present moment, as it is, all while adding struggle, drama, and pain to the facts of what is. How do we allow naturally occurring beauty and pain space to be there and then naturally pass, as all things do? Our insistence on controlling the uncontrollable can also get in the way of our openness to possibility and of noticing all the invisible pathways available to us if we only look, explore, and connect beyond what is immediately in front of us.

You've heard the saying that change is the only constant, and it's true. Fighting this is a reliable cause of suffering. Getting comfortable with uncertainty is key to comfort with risk, with change, and ultimately with growth.

Learning to work with fear is an essential element to rolling with the flow of life, and here we will dive into some practical strategies for embracing it (or at least, not letting it paralyze us). The ability to let go of the thoughts, people, and things that do not support our well-being at each phase of our lives is an essential piece to the puzzle of building enough resilience to stick with the changes you're making long enough for them to shift from "a new thing I'm trying" to "this is my actual life default setting."

FEAR IS NATURAL – LET'S DEAL WITH IT

Let's talk about the elephant in the room for every single human, no matter how superhuman we think we are: fear. It's hardwired into our brains to ensure our survival, but that doesn't mean we have to let it take over the place and shout over everyone else.

Goodreads says there are 276 books on the market right now with "fear" in the title. To call it one of the primary and universal challenges of our lives would be an understatement. My personal favorite is called simply *Fear* by Thich Nhat Hanh, a world-famous Buddhist commonly regarded as the father of mindfulness. His writing is so loving, clear, and accessible, and I've learned so much from him.

The dictionary defines fear as an unpleasant emotion caused by the belief that someone or something is dangerous, likely to cause pain, or a threat. Humans are pros at fear; our brains want nothing more than to ensure we live to see another day.

In working with clients, one of the things I talk about is how to work with fear, which is the universal way our brains help keep us safe (and sometimes hold us back from living full-bodied lives by keeping us small). We have fears of being seen, not being seen, being wrong, being judged—the list goes on.

Our ancient animal brains equated social rejection with a threat to survival. Being shunned from the community was dangerous, and so we evolved to fear judgment from others.

Nowadays, for people lucky enough not to live under dictatorships and in communities where their basic life needs are being met, being judged or ridiculed is no longer literally a life-or-death affair. These two facts are somewhat at odds but are both true:

1. You will be judged no matter what you do, so you may as well do what matters to you. Far better to be judged while living your best life than hustling hard to conform and still being vilified. No question.

2. Most people don't give much of a hoot about you anyway.
   This does not mean people are nasty; most of the time, we're stuck in our own heads and lives so much that we're not laser-focused on the foibles of everyone else.

Sure, folks may laugh if you do something ridiculously embarrassing, like trying to slide into home base on your softball team in high school, only to not make it and be tagged "out" just a few feet from the plate. (Yes, that was me. And yes, I did cry. And yes, my team was cool about it, thank God.)

When you said that dumb thing in your team meeting, some people may have laughed about it that night at dinner with their families, but then they forgot and got back to their own lives. Some people didn't even notice because while you were talking they were thinking things like "Why did I wear these ugly, squeaky shoes?" or "Did I put on deodorant?" or "I wonder if our neighbors will report our unper-mitted hot tub to the City?" Chances are, you've zoned out with similar thoughts.

Literally the only super embarrassing thing I've witnessed someone else do in my entire life that I actually remember (and will never forget) was that unfortunate time during Zoom pandemic-era public hearings when a commissioner of a board my housing development team was presenting to apparently didn't realize his camera was on whilst taking care of his morning constitutional in the bathroom. How did the Zoom facilitator not remove him from the meeting before everything unfolded on live stream public access television? Do they not like him? What happened to this poor man? Did he flee the country? So many questions.

Chances are you've never done that, and as long as you keep your computer out of the bathroom you should be in the clear for years to come.

Whenever I do something ridiculous it's oddly comforting to think: "Well, I've never done that." And frankly, I'm sure even that guy got past it and moved on with his life—if he can, so can we.

The moral of the story is that when (not if) you do something others find funny or objectionable, and you are judged, criticized, scorned, etc., there are only two questions to ask yourself: "Is the person offering this feedback someone I respect and who respects me?" and "If I put my ego away for a moment, might they have a point?"

If *yes*, take a moment to see if there are any nuggets of educational value you might chew on or blind spots being revealed and take what is useful. If *no*, toss the unwanted feedback straight into the mental trash bin we talked about earlier. Just because someone is serving shit sandwiches for lunch doesn't mean we need to scarf them down.

HOW TO WORK WITH F.E.A.R.

F: Forgiveness

Holding onto past hurts and the sadness, guilt, and rage associated with them weighs us down and clouds our perceptions of the world. Often, we are afraid to forgive since we feel it lets the perpetrator "off the hook." But our primary responsibility is to our own well-being.

Forgiveness frees us. It releases our energy to focus on all the good things we wish to invite into our lives. It also allows us in turn to forgive ourselves for the hurt we have caused to others at various points in our lives, whether intentional or not. Not only that, but forgiveness releases us from fear of judgment since we're no longer keeping track of who did what, when, why, and how. We can freely engage with others and the world, without playing small to avoid criticism at all costs.

One of my clients recently turned me on to the excellent book *The Seat of the Soul* by Gary Zukav. In it, he acknowledges that forgiveness sometimes comes really hard if the hurt is deep. In cases like these, he says it's enough to ask for the grace, the perception, and the elevated light to move toward it. I find this nonbinary approach of ease so comforting and useful.

E: Equanimity

Equanimity means mental calmness, composure, and evenness of temper, especially in difficult situations. If we can practice nonreactivity, we strengthen our ability to meet life's challenges with enough grace to respond intentionally, rather than running away or avoiding the issue. We don't allow fear to dictate hasty reactions that work against our well-being and harm our relationships with others.

A: Abundance

Having an abundance mindset (instead of a scarcity mindset) means we lean toward faith that we will have what we need when we need it. This removes the need to live in fear for survival. It is appreciation of life in its fullness, and joy and strength of mind, body, and soul. It is awareness that there is enough for everyone, and we can learn to give and receive with ease.

R: Release

Letting go is a skill we can practice. We can learn what lessons are available from situations and release the details and the mental wrestling with "how it could have been." It is a constant process of welcoming in new thoughts, practices, and learnings that support our well-being, and releasing attachment to thoughts, habits, people, and things that do not serve us. Fear of uncertainty and change causes us to cling—even to unhealthy situations (the known devil). A willingness to experiment and choose what works best for us takes courage.

A STRATEGY FOR REFRAMING FEAR TOWARD EXCITEMENT

Although our bodies signal fear and excitement in similar ways, these emotions are quite different. By tuning into this distinction in how we think about them, we can help ourselves lean into our exciting growth edges and keep safely away from what is not useful for us (and know how to tell the difference).

Fear feels like racing pulse, tight chest, an upset stomach, etc. We feel dread and the urge to distance ourselves for safety's sake. Excitement also feels like racing pulse, tight chest, and an upset stomach. But instead of (or maybe alongside!) dread, there's also an inkling of curiosity, energy, and the desire to explore.

We can be scared to try something new and at the same time want to try it, risks and all.

LESSONS FROM NATURE

Extreme weather events have become more and more common around the world and our home in Northern California is no exception. After years of drought and horrible wildfires, we had a record stormy and rainy season. Great for the rivers, reservoirs, and groundwater, but tough on the semi-dead, drought-stricken trees, many of which blew over in the seventy mph winds, taking out power lines, sometimes for days.

Having no power at our house for a few days was very cold and not much fun but was mostly manageable, and the quiet candlelit evenings eating Mountain Mike's pizza and playing dominoes as a family were actually pretty lovely. Wild weather along with a dental emergency, though, created enough disruption to knock me off my helpful routine—the stuff I've learned over the years keeps me mostly sane, centered, and nourished amid the stormy seas of life.

After a couple weeks of these events dragging on, I felt like shit and woke up one morning feeling worse than I had in a long time and unmotivated to do literally anything. The good news was that I'd been to this rodeo many times before, and I'd grown faster at catching myself before I fell too far down, so I could get back in the saddle.

My sister complimented my ability to identify when I'm veering off track and then jump right back into the rhythm and described it as an expression of self-love. I replied that it felt more like survival sometimes. Sometimes surviving is the greatest gift we can give ourselves, she told me. That's so true.

So, what's the formula for getting unstuck and back on track? I've learned it's as simple (and tough) as doing the next "right," "best" thing you can think of to regain movement and momentum.

I got up, put on my extremely unattractive Vibram 5-finger running shoes (yes, I realize this makes me seem like a minimal running cultist, and maybe I am?) and left the house for the muddy trails nearby.

Within thirty minutes, I felt restored to solid ground and spent the next hour getting lost in the muck and reconnecting to my body and my mental center. The cure for feeling blah, stuck, and out of sync was simply taking the next "right" (or right-seeming to me at the time, anyway) step.

In chapter 7, we created our morning habits stack and challenged ourselves to keep to it. Feeling balanced, healthy, and joyful depends on us incorporating these routines into our lives in reliable ways. It's even more important to keep our commitment to ourselves by actually doing them, even when it feels less convenient. Of course, there are times when life is truly too much to do our daily morning routine, and that's absolutely normal and A-okay. But if we've made it a true habit, most of the time we'll find a way to fit it in or get back to it after a setback.

When we're feeling out of sorts, and want to reconnect with our intuition, it helps to spend some time in quiet solitude—sitting, perhaps journaling, or going for a walk or run outside. If we allow ourselves the space to feel it, we'll know what we need to do to restore ourselves.

If we want to show up well for others (with patience, nurturing, and love), we need to do it for ourselves first. We can't give others what we don't know how to give ourselves. And the more we nourish ourselves, the more we can give to our loved ones, our work, and the world. I promise.

LEARNING TO LET GO IS ESSENTIAL TO SELF-POSSESSION

Karen Casey wrote an entire book of one-page vignettes on how to *Let Go Now* (and embrace detachment as a path to freedom). She hits this crucial issue from all angles until even stubborn-headed folks like me start to get the picture. One theme she raises has to do with where we see our center of personal power as residing: external or internal.

When we leave it to other people and material symbols of success to dictate our actions and validate us, we place our self-worth and personal power in their hands. We allow external factors we cannot control (such as other people's opinions or demands) to override our own sense of self and abdicate responsibility for ourselves in the process.

This ends up being awkward for both parties. *They* wonder why you don't have a strong enough sense of self to know your own value (and values). *You* keep upping the ante on your ever-more-impressive theatrics and achievements (oftentimes at odds with your true desires) to secure their approval.

The more we see that intentionally choosing our thoughts, habits, and actions is our number one job, the more easily we step into our power —and the less we default to giving our power away. From this solid foundation of self-knowledge and regard, we decide how to spend our time, energy, and resources based on what matters most in our lives.

We see that it's our job to give ourselves the love, encouragement, and acceptance that we crave. And finally, we come to understand that we won't be at peace, no matter how many "Atta gals" and brass rings we get, until we give these gifts to ourselves.

The best part? We don't have to put on a show or hustle for our own approval. We don't have to wait until we've achieved a certain level of personal evolution to be "worthy." We are worthy now, warts and all. We are all works in progress, and with any luck will keep learning and growing up to our last breath. This is what living an internal-values-driven life looks like. It knows that authentic personal power is inherent to each of us; it cannot be given to us by others and can also never truly be taken away.

REFLECTION ACTIVITIES

Reframing activity: Think of a time something "bad" happened and resulted in something "good" or unexpected or that resulted in learning and growth for you.

Example: I got laid off, but then found my dream job/new business.

What's a change you dread? List the worst things that could happen and ask yourself:

- Is there anything useful or productive you can do to mitigate risk or improve your chances at a favorable outcome?
- What elements of the situation can you impact with your effort?
- What cannot be controlled and needs to be let go?
- How might you practice flexibility of mindset?

Think about the same (or a different) important issue in your life. This time instead of asking what could go wrong, ask yourself what could go right? What would it look, feel, and be like if it all worked out? Describe this possibility in rich detail so you can really imagine what a positive outcome would be like. Our minds want to protect us from harm, and often spend an inordinate amount of time prepping for negative changes. It's helpful to spend time and energy on positive changes too, since whatever we focus on gets our energy and attention. Why not focus on the outcomes we want?

SUSTAINING PRACTICE: JOY

Joy is a net of love by which you can catch souls.
— Mother Teresa

This is the true joy in life, the being used for a purpose recognized by yourself as a mighty one; the being thoroughly worn out before you are thrown on the scrap heap; the being a force of nature instead of a feverish selfish little clod of ailments and grievances complaining that the world will not devote itself to making you happy.
— George Bernard Shaw

When I was in the depths of burnout and people would ask me what I did for fun, I thought: "What a dumb question. I barely have time to sleep." As far as I could tell, there were still plenty of necessary things on the list not getting done, so how on earth was I supposed to do a bunch of pointless stuff?

Sometimes we can get wrapped up in a fit of displeasure at the circumstances around us, angrily thinking something (or someone) else has to change. Then in a bolt of self-awareness we realize that, at least for now, the thing needing adjustment and attention in this situation is us. I've since been reminded how heartbreakingly essential fun, joy, and serendipity are to having a life worth living.

My mom was into this series of children's books called *Serendipity*; each has a sweet animal story and conveys a moral or value for living well. Serendipity means "the occurrence and development of events by chance in a happy or beneficial way." The stories express an optimistic sense of possibility, and I've always delighted in the notion that a serendipitous occurrence is simply one moment of awareness away. But many of us miss these simple moments all the time. All the mature, practical adulting we've been doing sucks all the fun out of us, and we develop a certain blindness to the whimsical delights of this world.

If you're out of the habit of experiencing joy, fun, and serendipity, the way to get it back into your life is through some good old intentional planning.

Wait, what? Planning isn't fun. How is this so?

That's because the people whose to-do lists chronically runneth over never put fun high enough on the list to actually make it happen—and if something fun ever does show up unannounced, you'll likely squash it or dismiss its importance, thinking of it as frivolous or a waste of your valuable time. I know that's how I felt for a while. Fun, right?

Okay. Let's get started.

THREE STEPS TO FUN

Step One: Invite joy in.

Determine what you like doing or creating; what lights you up; what you get sucked into and lose track of time with. What does this look like—feel like? Where are you? Who is there?

Feeling stuck? Think back on the last time you truly had fun. What was it? With whom? Where? Can you do it more? Or do some variation of it?

Note that this is not necessarily the same as what you are good at or what makes you feel productive or accomplished. In fact, how good you are is not terribly relevant to having fun. Practicing a "beginner's mindset" is a helpful way to embrace the fact that in order to ever get to the point of "good" at anything, you must first be willing to suck (which we all do at the start of anything new).

You can also invite more joy and fun into your life by practicing letting go of the "Four P's of Doom," which just get in the way.

- **Perfection**. How much fun can you have when you are sweating every detail looking for errors and ways things don't conform to plan? It's like inviting the cops to a high school house party. Allow yourself some space and grace to learn and grow—just as you would a child or dear friend. We're all messy works in progress, exploring all the way to the end.
- **People-pleasing**. This is one way we hustle to prove our worth, seeking external validation and hitching our happiness to that of others (which is not in our control). You can't *make* someone else happy even if you want to, so quit twisting yourself into a pretzel trying. Your job is to be yourself and to see to your own well-being and to share your light with the world as best you can. Let others walk their own paths and intersect with them in natural, mutually beneficial ways. If the real you is not their cup of tea, so be it. The equally important converse of this involves allowing others to be themselves, without trying to control, mold, or force them to conform to your liking.

- **Putting yourself last**. Also known as martyr syndrome. The only person whose well-being we are fully responsible for is our own, and abdicating responsibility for this is a form a self-sabotage. Get your needs, wants, joys, adventures, and passions *way* up high on your list of priorities. Lean into them, give them time and energy, and let them feed you. You'll be so much more fulfilled, and your happiness will spread like the sunrise to everyone around you.
- **Postponing joy.** We don't know how often or when the butterfly of joy will land on our shoulder. It's less than we would wish, and we're certainly never going to even notice it if we're in the habit of ignoring, downplaying, or dealing with it "later." Once the moment passes, it's gone. There is no later, at least not one that's guaranteed. Embrace moments of joy and magic as they arise. Also, not to be a downer, but none of us knows when our time is going to be up on this beautiful planet. Revel in all the delicious goodness you can when the opportunity arises.

Now that we've gotten the Four P's of Doom out of the way, let's do a quick brainstorming exercise and mine your imagination for a few more sparkling nuggets. For each question below, write down the first thing that comes to mind. This is meant to be a rapid fire, no self-censorship type of activity.

- What do you like to do alone? With family? With friends?
- What's something you liked as kid? A teen? A twenty-something?
- What's something cool you've been wanting to try? Another?
- How about something impractical? Something risky?
- What are you scared to try but still want to try anyway?
- What's something you'd like to try that is: near, far, free, expensive, quick, long-term?
- What's something you'd like to try that is: artistic, athletic, cerebral, outdoors, indoors, quiet, loud?

Hang on to this brainstorm, we'll get to it in a moment.

Step Two: Make space for lightness.

In the delightful book *The Art of Possibility: Transforming Professional and Personal Life* by Rosamund Stone Zander and Benjamin Zander, I love rule number 6, which is "Don't take yourself so goddamn seriously." Apparently, there are entire organizations that hold this as a shared value, and if anyone ever starts spooling up and losing their shit, someone else will call out: "Janet! Rule number 6!" And Janet will come back into herself, regain her mindful presence, thank the person for the kind reminder, and redirect her energy toward a more healthy and useful approach. The audiobook version is especially cool as it has musical interludes and their narrating voices are lovely.

I now have this written on my office white board so I can remind myself: most things that get my goat are not going to benefit from me hitting level 11 of intensity. When I'm really feeling grounded, I can often even find something funny (even if morbidly so) in situations.

Humor is one of life's most comforting elixirs, and it is free, helps others, and has no negative side effects!

Step Three: Nurture your unique, wonky, creative self.

Creativity is not optional. You are not born "creative" or not. We are all unique human beings with special gifts to offer the world and are at our best when we are offering what feels natural, glorious, and enjoyable. Creativity is how we express our true inner selves outwardly in the world, and it is essential to living fully and boldly.

Happily, imagination and creation are broadly defined. One need not be a classically trained painter to offer their creative energies to the world. Personally, I love playing my guitar, even though as a late learner, I'm not all that fabulous at it. Still, I've played for friends, family, at camping trips, weddings and funerals, and I even write my own songs. I used to jam with a group of ladies of certain age (we called ourselves the Hot Flashes) and have recently formed a new band with a couple of badass gals in my city. If you are not musically inclined, you may enjoy drawing, writing, painting, dancing, building, designing, coloring, gardening, acting, cooking, baking, knitting, fashion, etc. There are limitless ways we can make our ideas and inspiration manifest in the world.

Your challenge is to choose one. Go back to your brainstorm from Step One and circle the top five that stand out and resonate with you. Then choose just one to start with now.

Put it onto your calendar to do once a week for a month. If it's a long-term activity, just do one more step each time you revisit it. Then increase it to three to four times per week. Even ten to fifteen minutes a day will be enough to start to get a sense of how you like it. Give it a couple months before deciding whether you want to keep it as a habit on your schedule, or to move on to something else.

If you decide to try something else, that's cool. Keep trying things until you've found at least one thing you enjoy doing that cracks open the exploring/creating/fun-having part of your brain.

If you need more ideas and inspiration, google "Artist's Date Ideas" (based on *The Artist's Way* by Julia Cameron) and you'll find hundreds of ideas for artistic expression and fun things to do. Cameron calls taking yourself on a little creative date an "Artist's Date;" I love this. This book is, to my mind anyway, the most generous, gentle, inviting book I've ever read on acknowledging and nurturing the artist within all of us. It should really be called *The Human's Way*, IMO since it's about how to live from a place of deep connection with our intuition and gifts. And as such, it is relevant soul food for all of us.

DON'T POSTPONE JOY

I had a conversation with a new work acquaintance several years ago that has stuck with me in the way conversations do when they feel particularly timely, meaningful, and meant for you to hear. I was just about to set out on my sabbatical break from the working world—without a plan of what to do on the other side. He shared that a few years back he and his wife had lost a child at the age of fourteen. Perhaps he sensed my tendency toward wanting to find the "right" and "best" way to live (sometimes at the expense of living in the present moment in whatever form it takes). Perhaps he was simply moved to share some wisdom earned by living through his unspeakable pain.

He said simply: "Not everything is a problem to be solved" and "Don't postpone joy."

In the hustle of American work culture, where *everything* is indeed a problem to be solved (by hustling hard, sleeping when you're dead, buying a magic fix, and so on), and joy is *always* postponed in pursuit of climbing that ladder to nowhere, these statements feel at once obvious and incomprehensible.

Side note: You'll be dead a lot quicker if you don't sleep well and often. There are countless studies that show sleep is essential to mental and physical health as well as longevity. So cut the shit, hustle gurus, and take a nap.

As you prepare yourself for your new, lit-up life, make space to stop all the endless doing, striving, and mindless time-killing, even for a few hours, and allow yourself to notice simple moments of joy in your midst.

I came across a poem by one of my literary heroes, Mary Oliver, for the first time recently. It's called "Don't Hesitate." It feels especially appropriate in the cultural moment we are in, where the weight of the world can feel too heavy to bear, and burnout is at epidemic levels.

She reminds us it is possible (essential, even) to allow joy even in the midst of all of life's challenges. In it, she exhorts us to lean into joy whenever we sense its presence, after all, "joy is not made to be a crumb."

REFLECTION ACTIVITIES

Make your way through the Three Steps to Fun in this chapter and choose at least one fun thing to add to your life.

Take a little pocket jotter notebook and pen into the world with you. Capture ideas, inspiration, magic. Simply practice noticing details of people, plants, art, places, animals, etc. you would normally zoom by.

Read the poem "Don't Hesitate" by Mary Oliver.

CONCLUSION

You are the storyteller of your own life, and you can create your own legend, or not.
— Isabel Allende

You've reached the end of this guided journey out of the grind and into vibrant, 3-D living. Heartfelt congratulations to you! Burnout is the epidemic of our time, and it has been my absolute honor and privilege to share this journey and playbook for recovery from it with you.

It takes a lot of guts to pause, look within, and make lasting changes. It's hard, vulnerable, trailblazing work. But as brave souls like you know, the lifelong rewards exponentially outweigh the shorter-term discomfort that cutting a new path requires. I hope you've made great progress in your shift away from soul-crushing burnout, through self-care, and all the way to the magic of self-possession.

Just a short time ago, you started with learning about burnout then worked to make space in all realms of life. Then you rebuilt your schedule, mindsets, and habits, to support your well-being and ended with practice in sustaining your gains with a focus on resilience and joy. Now you get to decide your next steps toward soaking up all the richness this life has to offer and living into your own definition of a rich, full-bodied, joy-filled life.

That means it's time to celebrate! Here's a toast to you, your new beginning, and to a lifetime of energized, joyful, self-possessed living.

BRINGING IT ALL TOGETHER

Here are a few suggestions to help you really sink into this milestone and set yourself up for continued success.

First, take yourself out on a celebratory date! You've worked hard and invested a ton of time and energy, and now it's time to honor that. It could be a day at the river, the beach, in the forest, at an amusement park, a retreat center, or a spa. Perhaps treat yourself to a delicious dinner out with a loved one, a gorgeous new outfit that matches your reclaimed badass vibe, a trip somewhere special you've been wanting to explore, a new infrared sauna—whatever lights you up and leaves you nourished and refreshed.

Second, go back through your notes, journal, and exercises to reflect on your journey. Circle insights or themes that stand out or repeat and ponder a bit on how you might engage with those in the year to come.

Third, write yourself a note of congratulations and support for a job well done. Imagine the note is from a dear friend and think of what that person might say to you and the kind way they would phrase it. Imagine yourself drenched in love, compassion, and kindness as you write. Which habits, mindset shifts, and practices have best served you? What has helped support your well-being and brought joy and connection with yourself and others? Any creative insights? What are you proud of accomplishing during this time? What will you tell yourself when you're struggling?

Fourth, go back to your letter you wrote your future self from the introduction reflection activity. Read it and reflect on your progress and insights.

Finally, often clients find it useful to enlist the help of an accountability partner to remind them of their intrinsic worth and value and to help nudge them back on track when they inevitably veer off due to life's natural occurrences. The loss of a loved one, illness, travel, caregiving needs, work changes, or kids growing and needing varying forms of support are all examples of natural challenges and transitions that require extra time, thought, and energy from us, and can easily pull us out of rhythm. You well know by this point in your life that friendship is one of the most comforting and edifying balms there is. Lean on those you treasure, and allow them to lean on you. Think of who you might like to ask to help you in this way; perhaps you could reciprocate and support them in something they are working to incorporate into their lives.

WHAT'S NEXT?

The journey back to "regular" life after my recovery from burnout led through a solopreneurship; I launched my own real estate development consultancy and rebuilt my career with far more autonomy and purpose. By that point, the habits and mindset shifts I'd established, as well as my sense of self-possession, were solidified.

It's now been a while since I learned how to truly value and care for myself and the people and things that matter most to me, and though pressure has reasserted itself in various ways, as is natural in life, I've managed to continually find my way back to being centered in my own intuition and values each time.

As my clients recover from their burnout, they find themselves called to take different pathways based on their unique needs, goals, and dreams. Some will set boundaries and make adjustments in their current roles. Others will move to four-day work weeks or to new roles in companies that value their effort and have healthy work cultures. Some will start their own consulting or other types of businesses. And some will take an extended time away from work to allow for travel, time with family, a personal project, or a more in-depth exploration of possibilities for their next chapter.

It's my mission to help people step into their own self-possessed power, to go from burned out to lit up in their lives and careers and to reclaim their lives.

It's why I created a program called "Sabbatical in a Box," a fully resourced course to serve people recovering from burnout. It is what inspired this book. A friend of mine calls it "structured healing" since it gently guides you through the process of restoring yourself and cultivating a sabbatical-style mindset and way of being. It comes complete with a literal box filled with all the materials and delights you need to support the journey. You can find out more about this and my one-to-one and group coaching services, speaking and workshops on my website at CaraHouser.com

I hope that no matter what you do next, you take with you the learnings, mindsets, and habits we've practiced together here. May they serve and support you to sustain that beautifully empowered state of self-possession, where your choices and actions are your own and based on what's most important to you, and that your life story is of your own making.

Cheers to you and your fulfilling, sparkling, lit-up life!

A storybook we read to our kids a million times that I love so much to this day is called *The Big Orange Splot*. Mr. Plumbean, the protagonist, lives in a community where all the homes and gardens are the same. Neighbors describe it as a "neat street" and like it that way. One day, a bird flies by and for no reason at all drops a bucket of paint from the sky onto Mr. Plumbean's house.

Although he plans to repair the damage at first, Mr. Plumbean is ultimately inspired to keep the colorful splot and make his home and front yard into a tropical paradise, complete with palm trees and a pet alligator. He says: "My house is me, and I am it. My house is where I like to be, and it looks like all my dreams."

His neighbors are initially upset, but one by one they come by and drink lemonade with him in his garden and leave inspired to make their own houses look like all their dreams. The neighborhood is transformed into a beautiful, magical place where neighbors support each other in living and sharing their dreams. It is big hearted, generous, imaginative, accepting, and inspiring.

I hope this journey has offered you the inspiration, guidance, and resources to envision and begin to create a life that looks like all your dreams, and that you in turn share them with your loved ones, work, community, and the world beyond. The world needs your spark, and now is your time to shine.

REFLECTION ACTIVITIES

- Take yourself on a celebratory date!
- Go back through your notes, journal, and exercises to reflect on your journey.
- Write yourself a note of congratulations and support for a job well done.
- Go back to the letter you wrote yourself from the introduction reflection activity.

- Enlist the help of an accountability partner to help stay on track.
- Read the poems: "A New Beginning" by John O'Donohue and "Love After Love" by Derek Walcott.

REFERENCES & RESOURCES

INTRODUCTION

References

Fisher, Jen. "Workplace Burnout Survey. Burnout Without Borders." *Deloitte* (blog). https://www2.deloitte.com/us/en/pages/about-deloitte/articles/burnout-survey.html

Flynn, Jack. March 2023. "20+ Alarming Burnout Statistics [2023]: Stress and Lack of Motivation in the Workplace." *Zippa* (Research Summary). March 30, 2023. https://www.zippia.com/advice/burnout-statistics/

Gilbert, Elizabeth. *Eat. Pray. Love: One Woman's Search for Everything Across Italy, India and Indonesia.* (Riverhead Books, 2007).

Resources

Ware, Bronnie. *The Top Five Regrets of the Dying: A Life Transformed by the Dearly Departing.* (Hay House Inc., 2019).

CHAPTER 1

References

Garton, Eric. April 2017. "Employee Burnout Is a Problem with the Company, Not the Person." *Harvard Business Review.* April 6, 2017. https://hbr.org/2017/04/employee-burnout-is-a-problem-with-the-company-not-the-person

Resources

Pffeffer, Jeffrey. *Dying For a Paycheck: How Modern Management Harms Employee Health and Company Performance—and What We Can Do About It.* (Harper Collins India, 2018).

Kross, Ethan. *Chatter: The Voice in Our Head, Why It Matters, and How to Harness It.* (Crown; Reprint edition, 2022).

Nagoski, Emily and Amelia. *Burnout: The Secret to Unlocking the Stress Cycle.* (Random House Publishing Group; Reprint edition, 2020).

Neff Ph.D, Kristin. Self-compassion.org

Oliver, Mary. *Devotions: The Selected Poems of Mary Oliver.* "The Journey" *(pg 349-450)* and "Wild Geese" *(pg 347).* (Penguin Press, 2017).

Calm + insight timer mindfulness apps

CHAPTER 2

References

KonMari. https://konmari.com/

Magnusson, Margareta. *The Gentle Art of Swedish Death Cleaning: How to Free Yourself and Your Family from a Lifetime of Clutter (The Swedish Art of Living & Dying Series).* (Scribner; International Edition, 2018).

Resources

Carlin, George. "George Carlin Talks About 'Stuff.'" (May 2007). https://www.youtube.com/watch?v=MvgN5gCuLac

"Hymn of Healing." Beautiful Chorus. (Song)

Kondo, Marie. *The Life-Changing Magic of Tidying Up: The Japanese Art of Decluttering and Organizing.* (Ten Speed Press; First Edition, 2014).

CHAPTER 3

References

Bauer, M.D., Brent A. "What is an infrared sauna? Does it have health benefits?" *Mayo Clinic (Expert Answers).* June 11, 2022. https://www.-mayoclinic.org/healthy-lifestyle/consumer-health/expert-answers/infrared-sauna/faq-20057954

Burns, M.D., David D. *The Feeling Good Handbook: Using the New Mood Therapy in Everyday Life.* (William Morrow & Co; 1st edition, 1989).

Kabat-Zinn, Jon. *Full Catastrophe Living (Revised Edition): Using the Wisdom of Your Body and Mind to Face Stress, Pain, and Illness.* (Bantam, 2013).

Resources

Burns, M.D. David D. *When Panic Attacks: The New, Drug-Free Anxiety Therapy That Can Change Your Life.* (Harmony, 2007)

Celestine, Ph.D, "How to Change Self-Limiting Beliefs According to Psychology." *Positive Psychology.* November 24, 2015. https://positivepsychology.com/false-beliefs/

Hahn, Thich Nhat. *Fear: Essential Wisdom for Getting Through the Storm.* (HarperOne; Reprint edition, 2014).

Hahn, Thich Nhat. *How to Relax (Mindfulness Essentials).* (Parallax Press; Illustrated edition, 2015).

Hahn, Thich Nhat. *You Are Here: Discovering the Magic of the Present Moment.* (Shambhala; Reprint edition, 2010).

Manson, Mark. "How to Overcome Your Limiting Beliefs." Mark Manson Website (Article). MarkManson.net/limiting-beliefs

Neff, Ph.D, Kristin. www.self-compassion.org

CHAPTER 4

Resources

Tawwab, Nedra Glover. *Set Boundaries, Find Peace: A Guide to Reclaiming Yourself.* (TarcherPerigee, 2021).

CHAPTER 5

Resources

Chopra, Deepak. *Seven Spiritual Laws of Success: A Practical Guide to the Fulfillment of Your Dreams.* (ReadHowYouWant, 2009)

Dooley, Mike. "Notes from the Universe." *The Universe Talks.* www.tut.com

CHAPTER 6

References

Angelou, Maya. *Wouldn't Take Nothing for My Journey Now.* (Bantam; Reissue edition, 1994).

Dweck, Carol S. *Mindset: The New Psychology of Success.* (Random House Publishing Group; Reprint edition, 2007).

Muller, Wayne. *Sabbath: Finding Rest, Renewal, and Delight in Our Busy Lives.* (Random House Publishing Group; 1st edition, 2000).

Dalton-Smith, M.D., Saundra. "The 7 Types of Rest that Every Person Needs." Ideas.Ted.Com (January 6, 2021). https://ideas.ted.com/author/saundra-dalton-smith-md/

Merriam-Webster Dictionary. https://www.merriam-webster.com/dictionary/Sabbath

Resources

Casey, Karen. *Change Your Mind and Your Life Will Follow: 12 Simple Principles (Al-anon Book, Detachment Book, Fighting Addiction, for Readers of Let Go Now).* (Conari Press; Reprint edition, 2016).

Hahn, Thich Nhat. *How to Relax (Mindfulness Essentials).* (Parallax Press; Illustrated edition, 2015).

Rebecca, M. *Byron Katie's The Work Journal.* (Independently published, 2022).

CHAPTER 7

References

Cameron, Julia. *The Artist's Way: A Spiritual Path to Higher Creativity.* (Souvenir Press; Main edition, 2019).

Clear, James. *Atomic Habits: An Easy & Proven Way to Build Good Habits & Break Bad Ones.* (Avery; First Edition, 2018).

Dogg, Snoop. *From Crook to Cook: Platinum Recipes from Tha Boss Dogg's Kitchen.* (Chronicle Books, 2018).

Duhigg, Charles. *The Power of Habit: Why We Do What We Do in Life and Business* (Reprint, Library Binding).

Julia Cameron Live. "Morning Pages." https://juliacameronlive.com/basic-tools/morning-pages/

Mirreh, Mustafa. "Adults Spend 10 Years of Their Lives on Autopilot." *The Independent.* (September 28, 2022). independent.co.uk

Murphy, Jr., Bill. "Want to Succeed in Life? Ask for Forgiveness, Not Permission." (Inc.com, January 20, 2016).

Neff, Ph.D, Kristin. "Self-Compassion Guided Practices and Exercises." Dr. Kristin Neff (Website). https://self-compassion.org/category/exercises/#guided-meditations

Orlowski, Jeff. *The Social Dilemma*. Streaming, Netflix. (Exposure Labs, 2020.). https://www.thesocialdilemma.com/

Pelz, Dr. Mindy. https://drmindypelz.com/

CHAPTER 8

References

Casey, Karen. *Let Go Now: Embrace Detachment as a Path to Freedom.* (Conari Press, 2022).

Hahn, Thich Nhat. *Fear: Essential Wisdom for Getting Through the Storm.* (HarperOne; Reprint edition, 2014).

Zukav, Gary. *The Seat of the Soul: 25th Anniversary Edition with a Study Guide.* (Simon & Schuster; Anniversary edition, 2014).

Resources

Chodron, Pema. *Comfortable with Uncertainty: 108 Teachings on Cultivating Fearlessness and Compassion* (Shambhala, 2018).

Chodron, Pema. *When Things Fall Apart: Heart Advice for Difficult Times.* (Shambhala; Anniversary edition, 2016).

Doyle, Psy.D., Dr. Glenn. *Just So Ya Know:30 Things To Keep In Mind While Rebuilding Your Life.* (2021).

CHAPTER 9

References

Cameron, Julia. *The Artist's Way: A Spiritual Path to Higher Creativity.* (Souvenir Press; Main edition, 2019).

Oliver, Mary. *Devotions: The Selected Poems of Mary Oliver.* Page 73. (Penguin Press, 2017).

Zander, Rosamund Stone and Benjamin. *The Art of Possibility: Transforming Professional and Personal Life.* (Penguin Books; Reprint edition, 2002).

CONCLUSION

References

Pinkwater, Daniel Manus. *The Big Orange Splot.* (Scholastic Paperbacks; Reissue edition, 1993).

Resources

Altucher, James. *Choose Yourself!* (Independent Publishing, 2013).

Nepo, Mark. *Book of Awakening: Having the Life You Want by Being Present to the Life You Have (20th Anniversary Edition).* (Red Wheel; Twentieth Anniversary edition, 2020).

O'Donohue, John. *To Bless the Space Between Us: A Book of Blessings.* "A New Beginning" (Poem). (Doubleday; First Edition, 2008).

Walcott, Derek. *Study Guide: Love After Love by Derek Walcott (Super-Summary).* (Independently published, 2023).

Whyte, David. *Everything Is Waiting for You.* (Many Rivers Press; First Edition, 2003).

COMPILED REFLECTION ACTIVITIES

INTRODUCTION

Write yourself a letter, dated ten weeks out from now, about how you'll feel, who you'll be, and what you'll do after this journey. It is to be written in the past tense, as though these things have already come to pass. In your letter, describe:

- What you've learned, experienced, and applied to your life.
- The ways your life has been positively impacted and transformed.
- How you feel about yourself and the year to come.

CHAPTER 1

- Consider how you are feeling now. What does burnout look and feel like to you?
- Consider how you hope to feel by the end of this book. Jot your thoughts down.

- As you reflect on your life, take inventory of what's most important to you. How do your priorities and values align with how you spend your time?
- Read two poems by Mary Oliver: "The Journey" and "Wild Geese."

CHAPTER 2

Your turn to declutter!

- Choose a spot to tidy and a day and time to do it.
- Follow the steps above.
- Decide how you will nurture yourself after this. Decluttering can be quite a taxing process, and you'll want to plan to care for yourself after with rest or celebration or both.

Note how much lighter you feel after. Allow fresh thoughts and ideas to present themselves and when they do, note them! Gently get into the habit of noticing the ways your mind offers ideas and inspiration to you.

CHAPTER 3

- What activity might you do to help yourself create some mental space?
- When will you do this and for how long?
- What supportive practices might you investigate and experiment with?
- What self-imposed boundaries or limiting belief gremlins might be lurking beneath the surface? Take a look at them in the light of day and see if you can shift your thinking and be more supportive of yourself, your humanity, the fact that we're all learning and growing, and that most of what others say and do has nothing to do with us.

Here's another strategy for making mental space. I did this with my kids, and I now share it with clients, and it's called "glitter breathing." Some folks are more into mindfulness exercises than others. Some of my clients say the notion of it is rage inducing. For them, and everyone really, try this instead. I prefer to call it glitter breathing anyway, because it seems more fun and frankly is quite an accurate description of what it is.

Start with an old glass jar with a lid. Rinse thoroughly and remove the label. Put in a tablespoon or two of your favorite glitter color(s). Fill the rest with water and put on the lid. Shake liberally and watch the jar until all the glitter settles. Take deep breaths while watching and imagine your thoughts settling with each breath just like the glitter settles.

As your breathing settles, your thoughts will settle too, and at the end, you'll have done a couple minutes of relaxing deep breathing and calmed your nervous system. Keep it at your desk or wherever you like and repeat as needed.

CHAPTER 4

- Revisit the exercises and questions in this chapter. Any insights?
- What schedule changes can you make to ensure your time is being spent on what matters most?
- What promise can you keep to yourself?
- Identify an optional task you've been plugging along with that you really would rather not do. Practice saying no the next time it comes up.
- Think of a boundary you might want to establish and how you might announce it.
- Give yourself grace, credit, and a loving hug; this can be a scary and hard set of skills to practice.

CHAPTER 5

Here's a quick summary of the Fever Dream Time Machine activity. Details above.

- **Grab** a pen and paper or a computer. This should take you twenty to thirty minutes to complete, and you'll want a quiet, comfortable, uninterrupted space in which to do it.
- **Think** on the questions we raised earlier in the chapter.
- **Imagine** it's seven years into the future and write down everything you are doing in as much detail as you can.
- **Dream** big and do not censor or edit yourself in any way. Just keep going and writing down anything that comes into your stream of consciousness until nothing else comes out.
- **Create** something visual to represent the life you've imagined.

Then, set aside five minutes a day, either first thing in the morning or before you go to bed, to look at what you created and visualize yourself living this life using the handy Dos and Don'ts above.

CHAPTER 6

What's something you've always wanted to try but:

- You didn't think you could since you have no "innate talent."
- You thought it was too late or you're too old.
- You were told you were bad at it, so you never tried.
- You figured you'd never be able to learn due to some special level of incompetence, impatience, or embarrassment. (Why are we so mean to ourselves?)

What's something you have tried that you're kind of *meh* at but are now willing to put in the effort to improve?

What's one thing you've been grudgingly doing because you think you *should*, but it's not actually necessary and is weighing on you like a set of brass, 1980s shoulder pads?

What does sabbatical mean to you? What could it look like for you? Remember, sabbaticals can be small parts of your day instead of full-fledged escapes. How can you cultivate a sabbatical-style mindset and way of being into your everyday life by giving yourself the gifts of rest, recovery, restoration, rejuvenation, reconnection, and rejoicing?

CHAPTER 7

Ask yourself if what you're doing today is getting you closer to what you want to be doing tomorrow. What would your future self thank you for?

Map out your own morning routine habit stack and put it by your bed. Challenge yourself to stick with it for 30 days!

CHAPTER 8

Reframing activity: Think of a time something "bad" happened and resulted in something "good" or unexpected or that resulted in learning and growth for you.

Example: I got laid off, but then found my dream job/new business.

What's a change you dread? List the worst things that could happen and ask yourself:

- Is there anything useful or productive you can do to mitigate risk or improve your chances at a favorable outcome?
- What elements of the situation can you impact with your effort?
- What cannot be controlled and needs to be let go?
- How might you practice flexibility of mindset?

Think about the same (or a different) important issue in your life. This time instead of asking what could go wrong, ask yourself what could go right? What would it look, feel, and be like if it all worked out? Describe this possibility in rich detail so you can really imagine what a positive outcome would be like. Our minds want to protect us from harm, and often spend an inordinate amount of time prepping for negative changes. It's helpful to spend time and energy on positive changes too, since whatever we focus on gets our energy and attention. Why not focus on the outcomes we want?

CHAPTER 9

Make your way through the Three Steps to Fun in this chapter and choose at least one fun thing to add to your life.

Take a little pocket jotter notebook and pen into the world with you. Capture ideas, inspiration, magic. Simply practice noticing details of people, plants, art, places, animals, etc. you would normally zoom by.

Read the poem "Don't Hesitate" by Mary Oliver.

CONCLUSION

- Take yourself on a celebratory date!
- Go back through your notes, journal, and exercises to reflect on your journey.
- Write yourself a note of congratulations and support for a job well done.
- Go back to the letter you wrote yourself from the introduction reflection activity.
- Enlist the help of an accountability partner to help stay on track.
- Read the poems: "A New Beginning" by John O'Donohue and "Love After Love" by Derek Walcott.

ACKNOWLEDGEMENTS

The love and support of my family and friends has been instrumental in my recovery from burnout and reimagining a rich fulfilling life after hustle culture. I am beyond grateful and blessed to have you in my life.

Love and gratitude to my mom, who navigated countless challenges and did her best to give us a strong and healthy foundation with as much opportunity as possible.

My clients have entrusted me to walk with them along challenging parts of their journeys and I'm honored to have played a part in their transformations. They inspire me daily and I've learned so much from all of them.

My launch team is full of the most generous, creative souls, and their kind help during the book launch process was invaluable and has made all the difference. I deeply appreciate every one of them.

Stephanie Feger, founder of the emPower PR Group, has offered so much grace and encouragement, in addition to hard core technical expertise throughout the editing, publishing, and marketing journeys for this book.

Cara Steinmann, founder of the Ravel Collective, runs the most warm, welcoming, and genuinely connected networking organization I've ever experienced—the support of this community has meant the world to me.

Huge thanks to Jessie Patterson, my amazing coach and friend, for your unwavering faith in my ability to transform this dream into reality.

To the teachers, coaches, bosses, and mentors who have enlightened me, offered wise perspectives, and believed in me—I thank you.

And finally, I have been blessed beyond measure and thank God, creator, and universal spirit for all of the love and support I know has held, nurtured, and encouraged me throughout my life.

MY GIFT TO YOU

I envision this book becoming a dynamic, living resource for you as you navigate through burnout and reclaim your life. As you delve into the concepts shared throughout the book, not just now but when (or if) burnout tries to show up again, I'm delighted to provide you with a valuable tool—a Reflection Activity Workbook, yours to download and revisit whenever needed.

Visit www.CaraHouser.com to access your free Reflection Activity Workbook. It's designed to accompany you on your path toward self-possession, life-work balance, and crafting a lifestyle aligned with what matters most to you—one you don't need to escape from.

ABOUT THE AUTHOR

 Cara Houser spent twenty years learning how to survive and ultimately thrive in the ultra-male, pressure cooker real estate development business. During that time, her teams produced over 3,000 homes in the San Francisco Bay Area, creating over $1.5B in value. Now she is a career strategist and empowerment coach helping high impact women leaders step into their power and go from burned out to lit up in their lives and careers.

Cara was born and raised in Richmond, California, and earned her B.A. in political science from UC Berkeley. She loves traveling and adventures of all kinds, trail running, the coastal redwoods, relaxing by the fire at home with family and friends, and playing her guitar. She lives in El Cerrito, California (near San Francisco) with her husband and two teenagers, and after over four decades living in an often foggy climate, she finally likes it!

She also loves connecting with readers and helping others create their own lit-up lives. Ideas, feedback, questions?

Email her at hello@carahouser.com.

HOW CARA HOUSER CAN SUPPORT YOU

Ready to go from burned out to lit up?

Looking for thought partnership, strategic insight, and accountability to help you create true life-work balance (in that order) through career transitions like:

- Recovering from burnout and restoring your well-being
- Making the most of career advancement opportunities
- Developing your professional value proposition and story
- Getting back in the game after a layoff, on your own terms
- Exploring a new chapter when you're not sure what's next
- Growing into a promotion and the challenges that come with a new role
- Transitioning away from "employee" and building your own consulting solopreneurship

Cara Houser can help you where and how you need it.

Visit www.CaraHouser.com for more information on coaching, keynotes, workshops, and the Sabbatical in a Box course. You can also subscribe to her free newsletter there and receive a trove of resources.